Freemasons

FREEMASONS

Symbols, Rituals and Principles

MARCO CARINI

Bath New York Singapore Hong Kong Cologne Delhi Melbourne

This is a Parragon Publishing book.
This edition published in 2010.

Copyright © 2010 Parragon Books Ltd.
Queen Street House
4 Queen Street
Bath BA1 1HE, UK

Production: ditter.projektagentur GmbH
Project coordinator: Irina Ditter-Hilkens
Editor: Michael Konze
Picture editor: Barbara Linz
(Series) design: Claudio Martinez
DTP layout and composition: Malzkorn
Kommunikation & Gestaltung, Gerd Türke
Lithography: Klaussner Medien Service GmbH

English edition produced by
Cambridge Publishing Management Ltd
Translation: David Darrah-Morgan
Copy editor: Richard Gilbert
Proofreader: Hazel Meek

ISBN: 978-1-4075-8624-3

Printed in Spain

CONTENTS

The Inner Life of Freemasons ... 25

The Organization of the Freemasons ... 47

The History of Freemasonry ... 61

Freemasonry has a long tradition and has attracted many prominent members, including George Washington, the first US President.

WHAT IS FREEMASONRY?

Fraternity of men or dangerous secret society? Freemasons' lodges have existed for nearly 300 years, although their roots reach much further back into the past.

The Freemasons see themselves as a worldwide fraternal, friendly society of men that aspires toward shared human values and the positive and unfettered self-improvement of its members. Critics, however, often consign Freemasons to the category of obscure secret societies. They have been held responsible for conspiracies, assassinations, economic disasters, and even the outbreak of wars.

Secrecy and Mysterious Practices

Such views of the fraternity are nourished by the fact that every Freemason has to undertake not to reveal to the outside world anything about the inner life of his lodge. Folkloric costumes, strange customs, secret symbols, and mystic rituals all contribute toward outsiders' perception of the world of the Freemasons as alien, mysterious, and sworn to secrecy; even conspiratorial and threatening. Since time immemorial, Freemasons have been persecuted in many countries and are banned in some nations even today.

A Journey of Discovery into an Alien World

Dangerous or harmless? To answer this question, you must immerse yourself in the traditions of the Freemasons, find out more about their history, and learn to comprehend their world of symbols, rituals and rites—a thrilling journey of discovery that begins with the emergence of mankind in ancient times and ends in the twenty-first century.

Freemasonry is still banned today in some countries, while in others, membership of the fraternity is professed quite openly.

According to legend, Freemasonry is said to have its origins in the building of the Temple in Jerusalem, which was commissioned by King Solomon.

THE ORIGINS AND
FOUNDING OF
FREEMASONRY

THE EMERGENCE OF THE FREEMASONS: ORIGINS AND MYTHS

As part of the ongoing search for their mystical, philosophical, and organizational roots, the Freemasons look back as far as the origins of the earth. Their numerous traditions, rites, and symbols draw upon aspects of Biblical lore, mythical legends, great historical buildings, and ancient secret societies and cults.

An Aura of Glorious Tradition

Over time, diverse theories, myths, and legends have evolved about the historical roots of Freemasonry. Officially founded in 1717, the Freemasons have themselves contributed to these in a particular way. They have adopted for their own purposes many episodes from cultural and human history, as well as from ancient myths and biblical lore. These are intended to lend the society an aura of great tradition and glorious descent from mysterious origins.

The Egyptian pyramids, which came into being almost 5,000 years ago, are among the most impressive works of architectural art. The pyramid is for this reason still one of the most important symbols for international Freemasonry today.

From Creator to Kingdom

Freemasonic historians like the Scottish cleric James Anderson (circa 1684–1739) portray a legend of the origin of Freemasonry that begins with the "Great Architect" of the universe and the history of creation. The fig leaf worn by Adam in the Garden of Eden is interpreted as the precursor of the Masonic apron, and his son Cain is said to have been the first Mason. The myth tells that the first sciences were established before the biblical flood. The secret knowledge, immortalized on a pillar that was later found by a grandson of Noah, survived the flood. The teachings spread to Egypt and Babylon, and were disseminated further by Moses, the Babylonian King Nimrod, and later by the Greek mathematician Euclid. The first rules for builders are also said to have emerged at this time: Namely they were to show one another respect and to serve their lord faithfully. In addition, only the most capable were to be

Ancient pieces of evidence, like this fresco of a building craftsman from the twelfth century, repeatedly refer to the role that architecture has played in cultural history from time immemorial.

building of the Pyramids, the Roman Collegia, and the Druze religion. The influence of the Jewish Kabbalah, which is concerned with the mystical message of the Old Testament and the Talmudic religious laws, can also be discerned in Freemasonry. The most concrete historical references, however, can be traced in writings about the building of the Temple in Jerusalem, the Egyptian and Greek mystery schools, the Templar order, and the medieval cathedral masons' guilds. The Hiram legend associated with the building of the Temple continues to occupy a key place in the philosophy of the Freemasons even today. Many rites, symbols, and traditions of the mystery schools of antiquity, and those of the Order of Templars, were adopted by the Freemasons. Finally, the church masons' guilds directly gave rise to the first Freemasons' lodges.

appointed masters of building works, with background and wealth not playing any role. These customs ultimately also spread to Israel, where they flourished anew during the construction of the Temple in Jerusalem by King Solomon and his master builder Hiram. After its completion, the skilled builders dispersed and spread their knowledge via Persia, Greece, Rome, and France to England. Franks and Anglo-Saxons are also mentioned by Anderson in connection with the history of the stonemasons' fraternities. His chronology of Masonic prehistory closes with a discourse on the English kings and their links with architecture.

Secret Societies, Myths, and Church Masons' Guilds

Additional roots of Freemasonry that are repeatedly mentioned in Freemasonic literature include the

Euclid (circa 365–300 BC) was a Greek mathematician. According to the Freemasons, he brought geometry, the most important component of the builders' art, to Egypt, and disseminated knowledge of it there.

THE LEGEND OF HIRAM

One of the legends of the origins of Freemasonry that delves furthest back into the past is the tale of King Solomon and his master-builder, Hiram of Tyre. Hiram was in charge of the construction of the Temple in Jerusalem and was murdered prior to completion of the consecrated building by three of his journeymen.

Initiation from Degree to Degree

The rites and ideas of Freemasonry contain a great variety of references to the Hiram legend. Around 950 years before the birth of Christ, King Solomon summoned Hiram, an expert metal craftsman and architect, to his court to oversee the construction of the Temple in Jerusalem. According to tradition, the laborers at the building site were classified into three grades or degrees: Apprentices, journeymen, and masters. It was only possible for a laborer to move to a higher degree if he had been recommended and proposed, then

Pillars play a central role in the spiritual world of Freemasonry. Their significance derives from Boaz and Jachin, the two pillars in the porch of Solomon's Temple. They stand for the opposite poles inherent in every thing and every being.

Hiram's Death and Rebirth

In Freemasonry, the death of Hiram has to be re-enacted by every candidate to the third degree: that of Master Mason. The initiate, blindfold, is laid on the floor and wrapped in a blanket, and is then symbolically buried. Finally, the Master of the lodge whispers to the "dead person" the mysterious Master Mason's word. Through this ritual act, Hiram is reborn in the candidate, who is thus elevated to the degree of Master Mason.

selected for promotion to the next level, which eventually took place by means of a complicated initiation procedure.

Every Degree has its Own Secrets

The legend holds that members of each degree received their wages at a particular location. The apprentices received their salary at the Temple pillar carrying the name of Boaz, while the journeymen received theirs at the pillar called Jachin. In the Freemasons' world of spiritual ideas, these two pillars still represent the principle of two opposing poles, which pervades all aspects of life. Each degree also had its own level of knowledge and carried with it particular secrets, signs, and words. Apprentices, journeymen, and master masons each carried out different rituals during their work. Other special rites were performed when a "profane," a person new to the construction site, was admitted to the fraternity, that is, "initiated." All of these various traditions are still to be found in symbolic form in Freemasonry today.

Order as a Principle

The distinct hierarchical system that prevailed on the Temple construction site is another aspect of the story of Hiram on which Freemasonry draws. According to legend, the Queen of Sheba expressed a desire to see all of the laborers assembled in front of her; a single wave from Hiram is said to have sufficed for thousands of laborers to form themselves, as for a roll-call, in three ranks—one for each degree. The Queen was full of admiration for such impeccable organization.

The Hidden Knowledge

The legend of the killing and resurrection of Hiram also plays an important role for the Freemasons. Tradition has it that Hiram was beaten to death by three of his journeymen, to whom he had refused promotion to a higher degree. His murderers are said to have tried to extort the esoterica of the degree of Master Mason and the "secret word" from him, but Hiram remained silent. The word was lost, and the Temple therefore remained incomplete. Every Freemason is still searching for the hidden knowledge today.

The Inner Temple

The Freemasons see themselves as continuing the tradition of Hiram. However, they are no longer pursuing the goal of completing the Temple, rather that of constantly working on building the "inner temple" of

their own self-improvement. In doing so, they take the utmost care to recognize their own three "evil journeymen": Ambition, ignorance, and power.

According to biblical tradition, King Solomon ruled in Israel between circa 965 and 926 BC. He oversaw Jerusalem's expansion, had the first large Temple built there (according to tradition, the laborers on the temple building site were classified into three degrees), and opened the kingdom to foreign cultures and religions.

The Temple in Jerusalem, of which King Solomon oversaw the building in approximately 950 BC, lies at the heart of the Hiram myth. This, according to legend, was where classical Freemasonry, with its degrees and rituals, came into being.

THE MYSTERY CULTS OF ANTIQUITY

In the mystery ceremonies at Eleusis in Greece, represented here, the participants paid homage to the fertility goddess Demeter in processions that were conducted secretly. Aspects of this initiation rite were later incorporated into the rites of the Freemasons.

As previously mentioned, the origins of Freemasonry lie in the mystery cults of antiquity. The importance of initiation ceremonies, rites and symbols, and of safeguarding the secrets of clandestine societies is today, more than two thousand years later, still to be found in the Freemasons' lodges.

Initiation into Mythical Secrets

The mythical and esoteric roots of the Freemasons extend as far back as the mystery societies of antiquity. In the Mediterranean region, particularly in Egypt, Greece, and the Roman Empire, many mystery cults that paid homage to different deities were established in the first few centuries after the birth of Christ. Each mystery cult took as its starting point a myth (from the Greek *mythos*: "Word, speech, tale"): An imagery-filled tale based on numerous symbols, which have been common worldwide throughout history. Mystery tales—for example the Eleusinian Mysteries, the Egyptian legend of Osiris and the cult of Mithras in the Roman Empire— were central among these myths, and all of the secret societies revolved around initiation. Esoteric knowledge was imparted to the *mystai* (from the Greek *mystes*: "Initiate") upon their acceptance. This was meant to enable them to penetrate the earthly and the supernatural to a deeper level. The initiation ceremonies always extended over several days, eventually culminating in the actual initiation rite.

The Promise of Immortality

The *mystes* initiated in this way perceived himself as a holder of secret knowledge, and was able to see his own life as a link between earthly mortality and heavenly divinity. In these mystery cults, death was deemed to be merely a transitory point on the way to a new life; the initiate was attracted by the idea of the immortality of his soul. Since the traditional religions of antiquity made no such promise, this was a particularly appealing element of the mystery cults.

The ruins of the temple of Eleusis were uncovered just under 20 miles (30 kilometers) northwest of Athens. Today, they are a reminder of the Eleusinian Mysteries, the initiation in one of the most important cults—that of Demeter and Persephone—in Greek mythology.

The Vow of Silence

In ancient times, the betrayal of mysteries was punishable by the confiscation of all property, or even by death. Although nearly all the great (as well as the not-so-great) minds of ancient Athens had been initiated into the Eleusinian Mysteries, the secrets were so well guarded by the initiates that today very little is known about the content of the ceremony. The "sacred silence" was, however, also intended to strengthen the feeling of solidarity within the group and to give the initiate the feeling of possessing hidden knowledge.

The decline of the mystery cults ran in parallel with the rise of Christianity. The elevation of Christianity to the status of state religion by the Roman Emperor Theodosius the Great in AD 380 had a decisive influence on this trend.

However, many key elements of the mystery societies, such as the initiation and the vow of silence, are later to be found in Freemasonic rites. But the cults of antiquity

The Eleusinian Mysteries

The Eleusinian Mysteries played a large part in one of the most significant cults of antiquity. Until around the end of the fifth century AD, twice a year large processions of thousands of believers made their way to the village of Eleusis, which lies to the west of Athens, and spent days there paying homage to the fertility goddesses Demeter and Persephone. The form and content of the sacramental acts, which centered on sacrificial rites, prayers, and dances, were kept strictly secret from all non-initiates.

can only to a certain extent be regarded as the esoteric origin of Freemasonry, as there are no direct links between the traditions of the ancient secret societies and those of the lodges that began to emerge more than a thousand years later.

Burial place of the Knights Templar: The Order was persecuted in the early fourteenth century, particularly in France. Numerous Templars were tortured and killed, and the society was officially disbanded in 1312.

of Jerusalem. The Order, whose members lived in self-imposed poverty, soon grew to be of such importance that it was granted its own base in Jerusalem's royal palace. It was there that, prior to its destruction, the famous Temple of King Solomon had stood, which also gave the society of knights its name.

The Rise and Fall of the Order

The Order expanded rapidly in the Middle East and throughout Europe, and by the thirteenth century it had approximately 15,000 members. Since members had to transfer all their property to the Order, it soon accumulated vast riches. Its power and influence became so great that more and more princes and kings became politically and financially dependent on the Templars. The French King Philip IV, known as Philip the Fair, feared that the knights wanted to overthrow him and assume rule over France. He had the leader of the Templars, Jacques de Molay, and the majority of his supporters arrested in the early fourteenth century. Many of those incarcerated were forced to confess that they had committed blasphemous acts under torture. The brothers of the Order who stood accused of heresy were condemned in show trials and burnt at the stake. Their violent deaths sealed the downfall of the Templars.

THE LEGACY OF THE TEMPLARS

The medieval Order of the Knights Templar was violently crushed at the start of the fourteenth century. Some of its traditions reappear over 300 years later among the Freemasons.

Poor Knights

The Order of the Knights Templar, a secret society that was probably founded in 1118 by the French nobleman Hugues de Payens together with eight followers, was of key significance to Freemasonry. The aim of the society was to protect pilgrims making their way to the holy city

"Strict Observance"

In the middle of the eighteenth century, the German Baron Karl Gotthelf von Hund (1722–76) attempted to fuse Templar traditions with Freemasonry. The members of the so-called "Strict Observance" rite saw themselves as the direct successors of the Templars, and their highest degree of recognition was that of a Knight Templar. For a time the "Strict Observance" rite had more than 1,300 members, including no fewer than 26 German princes, and spread from Saxony into France, Russia, and Scandinavia. After Baron von Hund's death, the organization collapsed and was dissolved in 1782.

Templars and Masons

Since not all the Knights Templar were arrested and killed, numerous myths have grown up around their legacy. Some historians have been able to see a direct connection between them and the Freemasonic lodges founded four hundred years after the suppression of the Templars, seeing Freemasonry as the resurrection and revival of the destroyed order and its traditions. It is true that there are actually a number of parallels between the Templars and the Freemasons; for example, initiation rites and strictly guarded secrets play a major role in both. It is also a fact that the Freemasons took the term "Grand Master," for example, from the Knights Templar and have dedicated one of their higher degrees to the "legend of de Molay." Within Freemasonry there are also a number of rituals that hark back to the Templars, while insignia such as the square, plumb, and hammer, which are key symbols in Freemasonry, have also been found on the tombs and coffins of many Templars. However, the theory that the Freemasons are the legitimate heirs of the Knights Templar belongs in the realm of myth and legend, and is unlikely to ever be proven.

The Knights Templar, known for short as the Templars, was a medieval chivalric order. They were identifiable by their white tabard and red cross, the so-called *croix pattée*.

From Medieval Church Masons' Guild to Lodge

The actual forerunners of Freemasonry were the medieval church masons' guilds, which appeared wherever churches were being built. Their members comprised stonemasons, bricklayers, and roofers, who were connected with one another through secret knowledge and rituals. It is from these guilds that Freemasons' lodges were later to develop.

The Emergence of Church Masons' Guilds

From AD 1000 onward, churches and monasteries were being built all over western Europe, and wherever huge and grand cathedrals and minsters arose, the builders would band together to form craftsmen's associations. These so-called church masons' guilds were communities structured along strictly hierarchical lines. At the bottom were the ordinary stonemasons who often worked enormous blocks of stone. After their apprenticeship

In Freemasonry, the compasses stand for the tradition of architectural design. At the same time, they symbolize the intellectual and spiritual imperatives, and, for Freemasons, they also represent openness and tolerance.

Masons and Freemasons

The term "freemason"—a contraction of the term "freestone mason"—was first mentioned in a written document in 1376. It was used in the Middle Ages to designate a trained and qualified stonemason and church builder. It is impossible to clarify conclusively what specific activities were performed by the freemasons or how the meaning of the term has changed over the centuries.

There are, however, indications that the freemasons possessed sculpting qualifications and carried out the duties of an architect. It is also unclear what precisely the difference between a mason and a freemason was. In the fifteenth and sixteenth centuries the two terms were used synonymously.

they were allowed, as freestone masons, to produce vaulting ribs and ornamental embellishments to specific templates. Freestone masons progressed to become monumental sculptors, creating statues based on biblical models. The head of the church masons' guild was the master mason. He possessed the guild secrets and had the craft, technical, mathematical, and design knowledge that was indispensable for building a cathedral.

Sworn to a Secret

The building fraternities formed a sworn community who were held together not only by their knowledge as craftsmen, but also by defined rituals and symbols. All church masons' guilds had a book in which the design principles were recorded, a code of behavior that was binding on all the brethren, and a "secret": The inner guild.

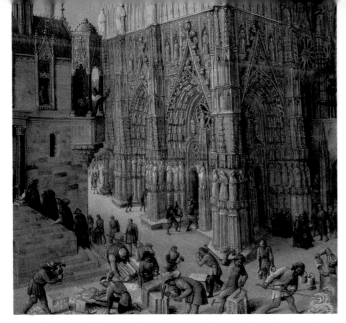

From about AD 1000 onward, numerous mighty cathedrals were built in Europe. Wherever churches appeared, craftsmen banded together to form church masons' guilds.

York Minster is England's largest medieval church. During the construction of this Gothic cathedral, the masons are believed to have organized themselves into a "lodge" for the first time in around 1350.

The secret consisted primarily of defined rituals, such as greeting formulae or passwords, by means of which craftsmen who were strangers could recognize one another and that served as a means of identification for wandering apprentices. In this way, the stonemasons' guilds guarded the secrets of their profession extremely carefully, so that no outsider could acquire knowledge of the guilds.

From Church Masons' Guild to Lodge

The mid-fifteenth century saw the start of the slow decline of the church masons' guilds. Fewer and fewer cathedrals and castles were being built, so the craftsmen's associations became less and less important. However, it took until well into the seventeenth century before the church masons' guilds were gradually dissolved, and in most cases, replaced by craftsmen's guilds. During this period the term "lodge," to denote all the stonemasons working on a building, appears. It was during the construction of York Minster at the end of the fourteenth century that the first mention was made of the "stonemasons of the lodge." The first documented use of the word "lodge" to denote an organized guild of stonemasons occurs in 1599.

The Accepted Masons

As the period of the building of the great cathedrals came to an end, so the structure of the lodges also

changed: Whereas until the seventeenth century they had consisted exclusively of members of the building trade, they began increasingly to open up to non-craftsmen.

The master masons enjoyed a high social standing, and people from outside the trade considered it an honor to be accepted into the lodges: Members of the nobility, the bourgeoisie, and academic scholars joined the masons' societies as "accepted" masons. At first, these honorary guests had no great influence on the work of the lodges. They did, however, bring considerable additional funds to the societies, which, because of their charitable duties to their own members, often found themselves in financial difficulties.

The Birth of Speculative Freemasonry

Over the decades, the ratio of craftsmen to non-craftsmen changed in many lodges. For example, in 1670 the Scottish lodge of Aberdeen listed just ten masons among its members, as against 39 men from professions outside the building trade. As a result of taking in "accepted" masons, more and more lodges changed from "operative" to "speculative" associations, in which the focus was no longer specifically on building work but on symbolic activities.

Thus, by the early seventeenth century, the original church masons' lodges had given way to clubs based on an interest in spiritual and social matters—modern Freemasonry had been born.

THE BIRTH OF FREEMASONRY

In June 1717, four Freemasons' lodges in London united to form a Grand Lodge. The merger heralded the start of a period of rapid development for Freemasonry. Soon, the nobility would take charge of the lodges.

Founded on St. John the Baptist's Day

The official date of the founding of Freemasonry is St. John the Baptist's Day, June 24, 1717. On this day, four lodges, named after the public houses in which they regularly met—the Apple Tree Tavern, the Goose and Gridiron Alehouse, the Crown Alehouse, and the Rummer and Grapes Tavern—came together for a

meeting in London. Only the latter lodge consisted solely of speculative Freemasons. The other three counted mainly builders and craftsmen among their members. The official reason for the meeting, which took place in the Goose and Gridiron Alehouse in St. Paul's Churchyard, was to unite the four lodges to form a Grand Lodge of London and Westminster, for the purposes of providing greater companionability. Another reason for the centralization was the acute crisis facing the three operative lodges, which were suffering from a sharp decline in membership. They wanted to merge with the successful speculative lodge at the Rummer and Grapes, which had around 70 members, more than the other three lodges put together. A further aim of the merger was to improve the way in which charity for the lodges' own members was organized.

The First Grand Masters and the Advent of the Nobility

The lodge brethren elected the oldest Lodge Master, Anthony Sayer (1672–1742) as the first Grand Master, but he held this office for only one year. In 1718, Sayer was replaced by a Secretary to the London Tax Office, George Payne, who in turn had to make way a year later for the natural philosopher John Theophilus Desaguliers (1683–1744). A short time later, Desaguliers, a member of the "Royal Society," London's renowned learned society for science, introduced the first nobleman to the lodge in the shape of the Duke of Montagu, who himself became Grand Master of the association of the London lodges in 1721.

The arrival of the Duke signified an enormous rise in prestige for the Freemasons. Increasing numbers of important and influential people now began to enter the Grand Lodge; from 1721 onward the Grand Lodge was headed exclusively by members of the royal family and the aristocracy, and went from strength to strength. For

On June 24, 1717, in the vicinity of St. Paul's cathedral in London, four lodges merged to form a Grand Lodge. This event is considered to mark the actual founding date of Freemasonry.

example, by 1721 the Grand Lodge oversaw 12 lodges, but just two years later this number had grown to as many as 52 constituent lodges.

Commission to draw up a Constitution

Before the founding of the Grand Lodge, each individual lodge had a "constitution" of its own, setting out its most important doctrines. In 1721, Desaguliers and Montagu commissioned the Scottish cleric Dr. James Anderson (1689–1739) to write a separate constitution for the Grand Lodge, based upon all of the others. These "Old Charges" were published in 1723 and are still seen today as the constitution of the Freemasons.

John, Duke of Montagu, was England's first aristocratic Freemason and was elected Grand Master of the Premier Grand Lodge in 1721. Under his leadership, the fraternity saw a large influx of new members.

John the Baptist and the Freemasons

John the Baptist, who administered the holy baptism of Jesus, has since time immemorial been the patron saint of the English stonemason fraternities. He is still considered by Freemasons today to be the embodiment of courage, morality, and idealism. His birthday, June 24, not only marks the date on which modern Freemasonry was founded, but still today remains the principal feast-day for almost all lodges. If possible, every Freemason is supposed to take part in this festival in order to show his membership of this global society. Since the date almost coincides with the summer solstice, St. John also stands for the light, which has a particular significance in Masonic philosophy. The three Freemasonic degrees of Entered Apprentice, Fellow Craft, and Master Mason—the "Craft" or "blue" degrees—are referred to in some countries as degrees of St. John, and the lodges conferring these degrees as St. John's lodges.

John the Baptist is seen in Christian teachings as the second-most-important saint after Mary, and as a model of asceticism. Besides Joseph and Mary, he is the only person to whom Jesus voluntarily submits (for his baptism).

THE SPREAD OF FREEMASONRY

Frederick the Great made a huge contribution to the rapid spread of Freemasonry in Germany during the eighteenth century. He was an avowed Freemason and actively promoted the fraternity.

Starting from Great Britain, Freemasonry proliferated not only on the European mainland but also in the English colonies. In the New World, its ideas fell on particularly fertile ground.

From the Island to the European Mainland

The publication of the "Old Charges" marked the end of the foundation phase of speculative Freemasonry, and it now began to spread into continental Europe. In 1729,

the first non-British lodge was founded in Madrid. In the years that followed, Freemasonic societies were established in Paris (1732), Florence (1733), the Hague, Lisbon and Stockholm (1735), and Geneva (1736). The first lodges were established in the colonies as early as 1729 in Gibraltar, in Calcutta the following year, and in Jamaica in 1739.

Frederick the Great as Patron

In Germany, the spread of Freemasonry is closely linked to the Prussian King Frederick II (1712–86). He had already been admitted to the Freemasons in Brunswick in 1738, two years before he ascended the throne, and when he became King in 1740 he officially declared his membership. On September 13 of the same year, the Grand Lodge *Zu den drei Weltkugeln* ("Of the three Globes") was founded in Berlin on his initiative. As the ruler of Prussia, Frederick led the way in promoting the admission of noblemen, senior military officers, and influential politicians to the lodges, which rapidly gained social influence as a result.

From Berlin, Freemasons' lodges spread first to Breslau, where a lodge was founded in 1741, and then to Vienna. The first lodge there, bearing the name *Zu den drei Kanonen* ("Of the three Canons") appeared in September 1742, but was only in existence for six months. In March 1743 it was broken up by the police on the orders of the then Archduchess of Austria, Maria Theresa (1717–80), as the future Empress distrusted the Freemasonic fraternities even though she herself was married to a Freemason.

The Influence of the Nobility

Meanwhile, the number of lodges continued to grow steadily in England, the mother country of speculative Freemasonry: From 52 lodges in 1725, the number had risen to 109 seven years later. In 1737, the prestige of the English system of lodges was enhanced considerably by the admission of Frederick, Prince of Wales, the first member of the English royal family to become a Freemason. However, the influence of the nobility on the lodges was not as pronounced as it was in England, Prussia, Austria, and elsewhere. In France, where the first Grand Lodge was founded in 1736, the promoters of Freemasonry were principally intellectuals drawn from cultural and scholarly circles.

Expansion in the United States

Through Scottish, English, and Irish immigrants, the philosophy of the Freemasons soon reached the New World. The pioneer spirit of the North American settlers overlapped with the creative ideas of the lodge brethren in many respects, and the New World provided a blank canvas on which the Freemasons' principles, which were based on tolerance and the recognition of universally valid human rights, could be tried out.

Franklin and the First Lodges

The first Freemasonic fraternities developed in the ports where the ships from Europe came in. The earliest lodges in the United States that can still be traced today were founded in 1730 in New York, New Jersey, and Philadelphia.

The first North American Grand Lodge, the St. John's Lodge, was founded in Boston, Massachusetts in 1733 under the aegis of the Grand Lodge of England, and later became the secret capital of Freemasons' lodges. The founding of numerous other lodges and local societies followed. The spread of Freemasonry in the US is inseparably linked with the name of American statesman Benjamin Franklin, who became a Freemason himself in 1731 and, three years later, became the Provincial Grand Master of Pennsylvania. In 1734, he also arranged for the publication of the Freemasonic "Constitution"—the "Old Charges."

Freemasons in the Army

During this same period, field or regimental lodges were established for the British Army serving in the colonies. Military personnel were constantly on the move, and carried the livery of their Order and other requisites in trunks. These lodges, uniting ordinary soldiers and high-ranking officers, were ratified not by the English but by the Irish Grand Lodge. The lodge system, and with it the ideas of Freemasonry, soon spread throughout the army. Large sections of the military leadership thus came into contact with Freemasonic ideals, which were to play a central role in North America's journey toward independence from England. One of these officers was the young George Washington, who was later to become the first US President.

As Archduchess of Austria, Maria Theresa ordered the dissolution of the first Freemasons' lodge of Vienna by the police. The future Empress distrusted the fraternities even though her husband, Duke Franz Stephan von Lothringen, was himself a Freemason.

THE INNER LIFE OF FREEMASONS

BETWEEN ETHICS AND ESOTERICISM

Freemasonry teaches that humanity is not abstract morality, but a practical philosophy of life. In the aspiring Freemason's personal growth process, great emphasis is placed on symbols and rituals.

If You Change Yourself, You Change the World

Freemasonic ethics do not constitute a closed philosophy. Freemasonry contains no dogma, rigid doctrine, or abstract moral teachings, but invokes humanitarian values that are conveyed through the community of brethren and by means of constantly recurring rituals. The aim is for the earthly/material and the intellectual/spiritual, represented by the principal symbols of the square and compasses, to be harmoniously combined. Thus the inner life of the lodges moves between ethics and esotericism. The idea of humanity pervades Freemasonic ethics.

Freemasons believe that they are building the temple of universal human kindness and worldwide brotherly peace, and this is reflected in their rituals. What matters to them is that they should improve themselves in order to go out into the world as better people, and to change it for the benefit of humanity. The path to humanity is a process of inner growth that is revealed to the Freemason, with the aid of symbols, through his ritual work.

The Misuse of Freemasonry for Business Purposes

The lodge is no place for wheeler-dealers. Attempting to benefit from Freemasonry for business purposes is frowned upon, and is considered anathema to the Masonic idea.

When submitting his application for admission, the new Mason must sign a declaration that he is not intent on gaining financially from the lodge. Any attempt by a brother to use the lodge to achieve personal economic or political goals is deemed to be an offense, and is punished.

A Freemason is further obligated not to show preference to a Masonic brother in business, as any resultant formation of cliques could damage the reputation of the lodge and its members. The quality of the offer alone must be the deciding factor and not the question of whether or not the business partner is a member of the fraternity. However, the boundaries are fluid, and the idea that business people who know and trust one another are more inclined to do business with one another than with strangers is no more alien to Freemasons than to non-Freemasons.

Joining hands in a worldwide chain of brotherly love: In the ethics of Freemasons, brotherliness and peaceful coexistence are paramount.

Help Among Brothers Must Not Be Self-Serving

What lies at the core of Masonic values and customs is Man as a suffering, loving, and, above all, learning being.

The essence of Man and his role in the community, the natural cycle, and the universe is one of the central questions of the fraternity.

Humanity, human dignity, empathy, and compassion are not just abstract virtues and imperatives, but, first and foremost, concrete practical concerns. Accordingly, Freemasonic ethics also include the postulated obligation upon brothers to provide reciprocal and altruistic help.

Misconceptions of Fraternal Solidarity

However, this fundamental principle has also brought the Freemasons into disrepute: It has repeatedly been alleged that Freemasons use the fraternity to secure business and other economic benefits. Secondly, there has for centuries been an enduring misconception that there was a rule according to which Freemasons could ask their brothers for help only three times, and then would be obliged to commit suicide. This rumor, which stems from the times in which men with an injured sense of honor actually did kill themselves, is devoid of any factual basis.

Nothing could be further from the intention of a humanist association whose paramount goal is the moral improvement of Man than driving its members to commit suicide.

The virtues of benevolence toward and willingness to help one's fellow man are central to the way in which the fraternity sees itself. All over the world, Freemasons are involved in the establishment of charitable institutions.

International Freemasons' meetings, like the one shown here in 1925 in London, are designed to foster the exchange of views between the brothers of various nations and continents, and to strengthen fraternal solidarity.

THE IMAGE OF MAN AND INNER GROWTH

Man and his self-improvement are at the core of Freemasonic philosophy. Accordingly, the highest purpose of Man's existence is essentially to work in order to grow as a person, and to have a positive influence on society.

From Rough Stone to Inner Temple

In Freemasonic philosophy, Man is compared to unworked "rough" stone. The stone can be formed into a personal work of art by constant "hewing." This process of shaping one's own life is also referred to as building the "inner temple." The aim is that through self-education, as well as through the fraternal bonds linking Freemasons, Man should recognize his true humanity.

The Great Architect

In the appeal to universal values and ideals, the extrasensory—transcendental—plays a key role in Freemasonry. The imperfection of Man is set against the allegory of the Great Architect of the Universe, as he is termed in the "Old Charges" of the Freemasons, who is not only the embodiment of a creator and protector of the world—while not being tied to any particular religion—but also stands for the principles of ethical responsibility and of works filled with wisdom and beauty. To approach this necessarily unattainable ideal step by step is the highest goal of Freemasonic self-improvement.

This copper engraving, dating from the middle of the eighteenth century, depicts a Freemason composed of the symbols of temple-building. These symbolize the various virtues that play an important role for the fraternity.

He should understand the most important values of a functioning community and organize his life accordingly. The goal is a new, improved human being. Upon entering a lodge, the newly admitted brother thus faces the task of self-improvement. Four values that are key to the way Freemasons see themselves are central: Freedom, tolerance, humanity, and fraternal solidarity.

Rituals Replace Rules

The Freemasons' way of life is consequently an ethical approach to Man's journey on the path to self-perfection. This practical, ethical approach has no strict rules or commandments. Instead, it makes use of practice and constant repetition to convey ideas of model behavior among the lodge brethren. This is also the purpose of the Freemasonic rituals undertaken by the fraternity in its so-called temple works.

All Men Become Brothers

Freemasonry sees itself as a university of tolerance and brotherliness, and through these ideals unites all of its members around the world. It allows each member to retain his own convictions and way of life; at the same time, however, it requires all brothers to commit themselves to striving for virtues that it considers important to people of all cultures, races, backgrounds, and creeds. The image of Man is consequently both unifying and equalizing.

The Freemason's image of Man is defined by the idea of the individual's constant search for self-perfection and by his influence on the human community, in which he strives for equality. Every lodge brother is also helping to build the temple of universal human kindness, engendering a more humane society. The implementation of Freemasonic values and ideals in society is the responsibility of each individual, but the guiding principle of Freemasonic ethics is the solidarity and fellowship of Mankind—the unification of all men within the greater family of humanity, the "chain of brothers" that spans the world. Based upon this fundamental idea, Freemasons have established many charities and aid organizations, and have also worked to achieve peaceful solutions to global problems.

Man as rough stone that needs to be hewn artistically: What is being done here externally to the likeness of Abraham Lincoln during the creation of the Mount Rushmore Memorial, Freemasons strive to achieve internally, through self-education.

FREEDOM AND TOLERANCE

Freemasons believe that freedom and tolerance are codependent: Only someone who respects a person who thinks differently from them will not restrict that person's liberty. Rather than a person's worldview and beliefs, what matters to a Freemason is their honor and honesty. This aims to achieve the development of a brotherly community free from prescriptive thinking.

Tolerance Means Respect for Others

Freemasonry played a decisive role in spreading ideas of tolerance. The term "tolerance" was borrowed in the sixteenth century from the Latin word *tolerare* in its meaning of "endure," "put up with," or "allow." But for Freemasons it means even more: Different, deviating opinions and lifestyles should not only be put up with or endured, but also esteemed and respected. For Freemasons, tolerance is based on the recognition that no man is in possession of the absolute truth, because no such truth exists. It is thus not a man's convictions or his beliefs that are the decisive factors in any assessment of him, only his honor and honesty.

This tolerance toward other worldviews and religions remains a key principle of Freemasonry today. It is perhaps best described by the summation of the views of the famous French philosopher Voltaire (1694–1778), himself a Freemason, on freedom of thought and expression: "I disapprove of what you say but I will defend to the death your right to say it." The Freemasons' aim is to bring people of very different religious persuasions and political convictions together in an "alliance of friendship." Their utopia is one in which "all men become brothers."

Art often hints at a link between Freemasonry and the attainment of civil rights and liberties. The Freemasonic symbol of the "all-seeing eye" is incorporated in this picture, which symbolizes the French "Declaration of the Rights of Man and of the Citizen" of 1789.

Racism, as practiced and encouraged by the infamous Ku Klux Klan, is alien to Freemasons. They are openly opposed to the Klan. However, even among Freemasons, the acceptance of black people was contested for many years, particularly in the United States.

The Freedom of Others

Tolerance forms the basis of the Freemasons' notion of freedom. The socialist Rosa Luxemburg (1870–1919) coined the famous sentence: "Freedom is always and exclusively freedom for the one who thinks differently." This means that people cannot be free while they restrict the freedom of their fellow human beings. No one can claim tolerance for his own freedom while not granting the same to others. However, it also means that tolerance is revoked if the actions of the other in turn infringe freedom. Freemasons everywhere must fight against intolerant attitudes and behavior, or at the very least reject them.

Human Dignity is Indivisible

The idea of tolerance and freedom is reflected in many fundamental principles of civil society. It is from these values that principles of freedom of conscience and freedom of expression developed, as did ideas of human dignity, and of inalienable human rights.

Freemasonic tolerance and its insistence on freedom rejects any discrimination against people on the grounds of their origin, their gender, their religious affiliation, or the color of their skin. It counters these prejudices with the principle of universal equality. On this basis, humanity and human dignity lie at the heart of all that Freemasons think and do.

The Principle of Tolerance

The principle of tolerance plays a key role in many Freemasonic rituals for Fellow Crafts and Entered Apprentices. Through the rituals, the Freemason is meant to learn not to see "otherness" as negative. He is encouraged to understand that it is the very diversity of ideas, beliefs, and practices that forms the basis of life's richness.

THE CONSTITUTIONS OF THE FREE-MASONS.

CONTAINING THE

History, Charges, Regulations, &c. of that most Ancient and Right Worshipful FRATERNITY.

For the Use of the LODGES.

LONDON Printed; *Anno* 5723.
Re-printed in *Philadelphia* by special Order, for the Use of the Brethren in *NORTH-AMERICA*.
In the Year of Masonry 5734, *Anno Domini* 1734.

Cover of the original English edition of James Anderson's *Book of Constitutions*, which appeared in 1723. The so-called "Old Charges" became the bible of Freemasonry.

The Most Important Virtues

The "first charge" reinterprets religion as a list of virtues that no longer have their rationale in standards set by God. The most important positive qualities are given as truthfulness, integrity, honor, and friendship. The "second charge" also lists peaceableness and loyalty to the state and its laws. The remaining four charges—based around the workings of the lodge and the behavior of its members—are predicated on these moral values.

THE OLD CHARGES

The rules and laws of the Freemasonic fraternities in Great Britain were originally so well guarded that they were scarcely known to outsiders. Only when the Scottish cleric James Anderson, commissioned by the London Grand Lodge, published the *Book of Constitutions* in January 1723 did they become available for everyone to consult. The "Old Charges" are today still considered to be the "Constitutions" of the Freemasons, to which their ethical ideas can be attributed.

A Religion for All Men

In his telling of the legend of the origin of Freemasonry, as well as in his list of virtues and charges, Anderson draws on numerous oral and written traditions, some of which are many centuries old. The tripartite division between religious, general, and craft rules is a longstanding one. "The Old Charges" (original title "The charges of a Free-Mason") is divided into six main sections. In the first section, "Concerning GOD and RELIGION," Freemasons are obligated not to the belief prevailing in their country or culture, but to a concept of religion in which "all Men agree, leaving their particular Opinions to themselves." Freemasons should believe in a god, but no one religion should be considered superior to another.

Rebellion is Proscribed

In the second "General Head" which carries the title "Of the CIVIL MAGISTRATE supreme and subordinate," any rebellion against the authority of the state is forsworn. If a lodge brother shows a rebellious attitude, "he is not to be countenanc'd in his Rebellion," but he may not be expelled from the lodge. The third section of the "Old Charges" deals with the subject "Of LODGES." Here, it is stated that "The persons admitted Members of a *Lodge* must be good and true Men, free-born, and of mature and discreet Age." Bondsmen and women are thus excluded from membership of a lodge, as are "immoral and scandalous men." Every Freemason has to belong to a lodge and act in accordance with its bylaws and general regulations.

The Rules of Advancement

"Of MASTERS, WARDENS, Fellows, and Apprentices" is the name of the fourth General Head of the *Book of Constitutions*. Here, the multi-level hierarchy within the lodges at that time is laid down: Apprentices can rise to become Fellow-Craftsmen, Fellow-Craftsmen to Wardens, Wardens to Masters, Masters to Grand Wardens, and Grand Wardens to Grand Masters; it is not possible to skip a level. For the next highest level to be attained, it is not age but solely the merits of the individual that should be the decisive factor for the lodge. The fifth General Head deals with the "Management of the CRAFT in working." It regulates the dealings of craftsmen with one another and their relationship to God and the laws of their country.

The virtues of integrity, politeness, and loyalty are central here. Finally, the closing passage, "Of BEHAVIOR," sets out the most important ways in which lodge brothers should behave toward one another, as well as toward members of other lodges and non-Masons.

The title page of the American first edition of the *Book of Constitutions* shows the first English Grand Master, the Duke of Montagu, handing over the "Old Charges" to his successor, the Duke of Wharton, in 1723.

RELIGION AND BELIEF

Freemasonry is not a religion. Despite its Christian tradition, it has opened itself increasingly to other religious orientations.

Religious Belief as a Principle

Freemasonry does not wish to compete with existing religious communities. It does not, as a rule, exclude anyone on the grounds of his faith or denomination, and emphasizes the necessity of belief in "a Supreme Being." The latter is referred to in Freemasonic philosophy as the "Great Architect of the Universe." On the other hand "stupid atheists," as they are termed in the "Old Charges," are refused admission.

When the United Grand Lodge of England was created in 1819, a new version of the Constitutions was drafted, in which the position was stated in this regard, "Let a man's religion or mode of worship be what it may, he is not excluded from the Order provided he believe in the glorious Architect of heaven and earth, and practise the sacred duties of morality."

In the art of the Freemasons, religious motifs play an important role. Figures from the world's religions, usually from the Christian faith, are to be found side by side with Freemasonic symbolism.

A Bridge Between the World's Religions

By stressing positive values such as friendship, humanity, and tolerance, Freemasonry endeavors to build a bridge between religions and to identify the lowest common denominator to connect value systems. Freemasonry challenges the major world religions, which it perceives to be dogmatic and intransigent, with an open system of religious belief and brotherly love.

However, these principles have repeatedly been called into question. For example, most German lodges in the eighteenth century took the viewpoint that only Christians could be lodge brothers, a stance which is still common today in some German and Scandinavian lodges. Most Freemasons' lodges, however, accept people of any creed, irrespective of whether they are Muslim, Buddhist, Christian, Jewish, or of any other religious persuasion.

No Obligation to Believe

French Freemasonry has followed quite a different course. There, the *Grand Orient* Grand Lodge removed the phrase "Great Architect of the Universe" from its articles in 1877, and started unreservedly accepting atheists. The *Grand Orient* justified this step by saying that it was necessary to emphasize the unconditional freedom of conscience of Freemasons. It was therefore impossible to prescribe that the brothers should believe in a deity. The removal of the wording "Great Architect of the Universe" caused a great schism between English and French Freemasonry. The English Grand Lodge severed relations with the *Grand Orient* and refused to recognize it.

Freemasons and Jews

Invoking their Christian tradition, the lodges in Germany and many other countries refused to accept Jews as brethren for many years. The *Loge zum flammenden Stern* ("Blazing Star Lodge"), which was founded in 1783 and not recognized by any Grand Lodge, was the first German fraternity to admit Jews, although only for a very short period. When Duke Ferdinand of Brunswick agreed to recognize the lodge on condition that the Jewish brethren be expelled from it, they had to leave again. It was only when Germans of Jewish faith were accepted into the Freemasons' society in France and subsequently founded a lodge together with German Freemasons in the city of Frankfurt that the divisive front against Jews that existed within Freemasonry began to crumble. The *Loge zur aufgehenden Morgenröthe* ("Lodge of the Nascent Dawn"), established at the start of the nineteenth century, was not, however, recognized by any Grand Lodge. Nonetheless, the fact that respected Jewish personalities such as the authors Berthold Auerbach (1812–82) and Ludwig Börne (1786–1837) were active members of it led to Freemasonry increasingly sanctioning Jewish brethren.

In the middle of the nineteenth century, the Grand Lodge of Hamburg finally declared itself ready to admit Jews. Other Grand Lodges, for example *Der Eklektische Bund* ("The Eclectic Union") took many more years before they were ready to allow "free and honest men" of Jewish faith to wear their lodge insignia.

The German novelist Berthold Auerbach (1812–82) was one of the first prominent Jews to be admitted into a Freemasons' lodge.

ESOTERICISM AND ALCHEMY

Alongside its system of values, esoteric ideas play a fundamental role in Freemasonry, and the lodges' formal ceremonies are characterized by numerous mystical rituals. These rituals are designed to give the brethren, on their pathway to self-perfection, spiritual experiences that could never be grasped by the intellect alone.

The Search for the Hidden Knowledge

In Freemasonry, together with the Masonic tradition and a system of ethics based on humanitarian and religious values, esotericism plays an important role. The word comes from the Greek and means "inwardly oriented."

Esotericism refers to rites, customs, and symbols used by initiates and not known to outsiders. In Freemasonry, esotericism is defined in particular as the search for hidden knowledge that cannot be attained through the intellect alone. What matters to the fraternity is not the imparting of "secret knowledge," rather self-awareness and self-development. Esotericism in the sense of a "secret teaching" is not part of Freemasonry.

The Rites of Initiation

The esoteric core of lodge work is above all else based around the large number of mystical rites associated with "initiation," which every brother has to pass through to reach a higher Freemasonic degree. In his search for knowledge, the seeker embarks on a mystical journey.

The entry of a "profane" into the lodge is associated with such initiation rites, which are characterized by their heavily symbolic content. As previously discussed, many of these rites and symbols have been adopted

Inwardly oriented, listening inside yourself: For Freemasons, the search for hidden knowledge begins within themselves.

Hermeticism and Alchemy

Freemasonic esotericism harks back to the traditions of Hermeticism and alchemy. Hermeticism is a tradition of secret knowledge that can be traced back to the Egyptian god of wisdom, Thoth, designed to help the seeker of spiritual enlightenment to acquire extensive and profound knowledge. The central Hermetic writings are primarily based on the philosophical schools of ancient Greece. One of the most important disciplines of Hermeticism is alchemy, from which modern chemistry evolved. Alchemy is concerned with transforming and ennobling substances and, in a metaphorical sense, the doctrine of the ennobling of man. The goal is full spiritual maturity, understanding, and immortality, the symbol of which is the "philosopher's stone." The alchemist's tradition is directly reflected in Freemasonry in the striving for self-perfection and in the allegory of working the "rough stone."

from the mystery cults of antiquity, the medieval secret societies, and the traditions of the church masons' guilds.

Experiences for Which there are No Words

Access to greater knowledge of the spiritual experiences of Man and his striving for self-perfection, his position in the universe created by the "Great Architect," and his place in the chain of Freemasonic tradition, are among the aims of the fraternity's esotericism. The esoteric rites provide Freemasons with spiritual and emotional experiences that are neither explicable nor comprehensible in purely intellectual terms.

A Freemasonic Master once expressed this as follows: "Previously I knew quite definitely how everything was. But when I then stood in the circle of brethren and the blindfold was taken from my eyes, my heart was gripped. What I felt at that moment, I cannot put into words even for myself."

Initiation rite to attain the degree of Master Mason: The Fellow Craft has to pass numerous ritualized tests before he obtains the highest Craft degree.

RITUALS AND CEREMONIES

Allegorical rituals are at the heart of Freemasons' gatherings. Their purpose is to extend the awareness of the initiate and to reinforce the solidarity of the lodge, and, through their performance, moral and ethical lessons on the principles at the core of the fraternity are communicated.

The Method of Initiation

Rituals have a special significance in Freemasonry. Central to these is initiation. The uninitiated are admitted to the lodge, and brothers are initiated to the next degree, through symbolic acts. This is not meant to happen through words and their intellectual processing alone: The fundamental idea behind the method of initiation is that it generates an intense interaction between the emotions of the participating brother and the symbolism of Freemasonry.

The Goal is "Inner Renewal"

Rituals, as Freemasons understand them, are dramatically staged sequences of set allegorical acts. Their central theme is that of a personal rapprochement to three existential themes. These are: "Who am I?," "The individual in his environment," and "Experiencing one's own death." Each ritual here has a clearly defined structure. First, the participant is put into the right frame of mind, then a symbolic scene is set for the event about to take place. The participating brother then undergoes the main part of the initiation, before the ceremony is brought to its conclusion by the dismantling

The signet ring of the Freemasons is one of the numerous trappings with which the members of the fraternity adorn themselves and by which they are able to recognize one another.

The acceptance of a new brother by the Freemasons takes the form of a ceremonial ritual. Upon his initiation, the "seeker," wrapped in white robes, is firstly led blindfold into a darkened room that is illuminated only by the flickering of a candle. He now finds himself alone in this "dark chamber," which is also referred to as the "chamber of lost steps" or "chamber of reflection." After he has taken off the blindfold, he will see in the room various symbols of transience, such as a skull and an hourglass. These symbols are intended to convey to him the finite nature of his existence, the end of his life as a "non-initiate," and the prospect of spiritual rebirth as a Freemason. In the chamber, the seeker now has the opportunity to reflect for one last time on his decision to become a Freemason. If he perseveres in his intention, he must answer questions on his understanding of Freemasonry in the seclusion of the darkened room. He is then collected and led blindfold to another ceremonial trial, which is closely bound up with the elements of earth, fire, air, and water. Finally, the blindfold is removed from him—the new brother steps symbolically out of the darkness of the chamber and into the "light" of a new life experience.

of the symbolic scene. The goal is the "inner renewal" of the brother and the broadening of his awareness. For this, he must be ready to open his mind to the acts specified and to give himself over to them fully.

Rituals that Reinforce Brotherliness

The rituals also have the purpose of strengthening the bonds between the Freemasons. Such shared spiritual experiences are designed to reinforce the feelings of brotherliness. In Freemasonry, there are set core rituals that are prescribed for the subordinate lodges by the individual Grand Lodges. Depending on the type of Masonic teaching, these can be modified slightly within the constituent lodges and supplemented by an individual lodge's own special rituals. Most of these mystical ceremonies originate from the traditions of the church masons' guilds, or can be traced back to the mysteries of antiquity.

Signs and Symbols

Symbols, along with their variety of functions, play a key role in the world of Freemasonry. They are the most important means of expression in rituals, as well as being tools to provide practical help in everyday life, forming a bridge to the world beyond the rational. They also provide a link between lodges throughout the world.

Omnipresence of the Symbols

The Greek word *symbolon* approximates most closely to the English word "symbol" in its sense of a pictorially represented idea. The symbol is therefore not a copy of a concrete object but the pictorial representation of an abstract thought or value.

The interpretation of the symbols is a matter for the individual Freemason; there is no rule assigning an unambiguous and defined meaning to a symbol. However, within the fraternity there is a shared understanding of many of them.

For all Freemasons, the square can mean only one thing: Integrity. The magic number three orders the

The Symbolism of Tools

Gavel: Symbol of force and endurance, power and strength, and also a symbolic tool for the working of rough stone.

Trowel: Symbol of the degree of Fellow Craft and of the "hewn stone." With the aid of the trowel, each individual building block is bonded firmly to the next.

Tracing board: Symbol of the Master Mason degree. As a rule, it is decorated with a double cross with a St. Andrew's cross lying below that.

Apron: Symbol of innocence and chastity, but also an allegory for work and protection from injuries.

Plumb: Plumbs the depth of the conscience. It symbolizes rectitude and truthfulness.

Square: Stands for the material world, but also for just thought and action, "squaring" one's actions with all mankind.

Angle gauge: Symbol of conscientiousness. Its two legs stand for rights and duties.

Level and spirit level: Symbol of the equality of men and the subordination of privilege to humanity.

Compasses: Symbol of the all-embracing human tolerance, and openness of Freemasons. The compasses also stand—as a counter and supplement to the square—for the intellectual or spiritual.

Signs and symbols play an important role for Freemasons. Each item used has a meaning, but this is not definitively prescribed.

The square and compasses are not only the most important individual symbols of the fraternity; together, they also symbolize Freemasonry per se. The compasses represent spirituality, the square the material world.

The traditional dress of the Freemasons, consisting of sash, apron, white gloves, and other items of clothing, is worn by the brethren at all important ceremonies.

The Carpet

In the middle of the Freemasons' workroom, called the "temple," is a square carpet or a board, also called the tracing board.

Various symbols that belong to the initiation rites of the different Freemasonic degrees are represented on this important prop. The carpet has evolved from chalk drawings, which—in the early days of Freemasonry—were traced on the floor before the start of a meeting and later wiped off again. The main motif of the carpet is the Temple of Solomon flanked by two pillars, with several steps leading up to its entrance.

The temple structure is surrounded by numerous important symbols of the fraternity, including square and compasses, hammer and nail, moon and sun. The seeker symbolically walks across the steps to the temple.

symbols: The as-yet rough stone or ashlar, the hewn stone or perfect ashlar, and the tracing board are the three "immovable jewels," while the square, level, and plumb constitute the "movable jewels."

The "three great lights" of Freemasonry consist of the Bible (or another volume of sacred law), the square, and the compasses. The "three lesser lights" comprise sun, moon, and the Master of the lodge—the "Worshipful Master." The two celestial bodies are seen as the incarnation of creative elementary forces, and the Worshipful Master as the "son," who radiates spiritual

light out of the lodge; all three serve as beacons to guide a brother on his journey, encouraging him in his struggle for self-perfection.

These and many other symbols, colors, and numbers, are ubiquitous in Freemasonry; they dominate the customs of the Masons, they adorn the so-called "tracing boards" of the three different degrees, and they appear in the coats of arms and seals of the lodges. They are present in Freemasonic paintings and embellish the medals, "jewels," which adorn the uniform of Freemasons.

THE SYMBOLISM OF COLORS AND NUMBERS

The tools of the mason and the architect are not the only symbols in Freemasonry: Geometric shapes, celestial bodies, flowers, colors, and numbers all constitute important symbols to the brothers.

Numbers of the Divine World

Freemasons believe that numbers have symbolic meanings. For example, three symbolizes esotericism and the divine world, but also the male and the perfect. Four stands for the material world. Five, made up of three and two, the latter standing for the female element, is the number of union; the rose has five petals, the hand five fingers, and man five senses. Seven is the number of mystical significance; the week has seven days and the rainbow seven colors. Nine is the master number: It is the square of three, therefore reinforces the sacred number; the Temple of Solomon has nine parts, and a mother carries her child for nine months.

Colors of Purity and Magic

Colors likewise possess a symbolic content in the Freemasonic world: Blue is the color of loyalty, of friendship, and of the universe. Gold is the symbol of perfection, of revelation, of the sun and of the shining light, but also of constancy and power. Green is the color of hope and mercy. It stands for new life. Violet is a magical color; it is the color of humility, penitence, and reflection. Red symbolizes love, while black represents mourning. Silver is the symbol of the night and of coolness, but also of life changes and of bringing forth life. It is the color of femininity and of the moon. White is seen as the symbol of purity and wisdom.

The "temple" of a Freemasons' lodge is the central meeting room. In it are arranged the most important symbols of the fraternity in accordance with established rules.

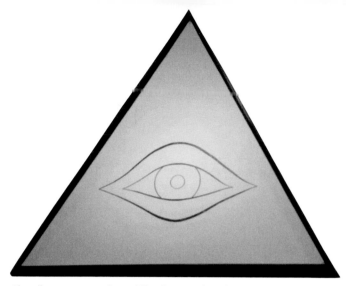

The all-seeing eye in the middle of a triangle or hovering above a pyramid is a symbol of the divine "Great Architect of the Universe."

The symbols of the brotherhood are also a hallmark of Freemasonic literature, a wide range of which is available worldwide.

Freemasonic Symbols from A to Z

All-seeing eye: a diffuse symbol that can be traced back to ancient Egyptian mythology, for Freemasons the eye in a triangle surrounded by radiating beams of light is a symbol for the "Great Architect of the Universe."

Blazing star: the highest symbol of transcendence represents the light that guides the Mason on his way, even through the most profound darkness.

Chain: the chain of brotherhood, which symbolically spans the globe, is an expression of international brotherly solidarity.

Checkered floor: an area composed of white and black squares, which symbolizes the idea that all contradictions are resolved in unity. The Temple in Jerusalem is said to have been furnished with such a mosaic floor.

G: in the center of the blazing star there is usually the letter G, which is open to a number of possible interpretations: Geometry, God, or "Great Architect of the Universe." In the Fellow Craft degree, Freemasons learn the meaning of this symbol.

Gloves: an important symbolic component of a Freemason's clothing, the gloves are a sign that the hands of a brother must remain clean when carrying out Masonic work.

Light: every Freemason is a "seeker of light," while those not yet initiated are wandering in the dark. Light is thus the symbol of initiation.

Pentagram: the five-pointed star is seen as a sign warding off demons. Just like its six-pointed brother, the hexagram, it appears in Freemasonry principally as a blazing star.

Perfect ashlar: corresponds to the Fellow Craft degree and stands for the stage of self-control.

Pillars: the two pillars that adorn the entrance area of the meeting room in lodges refer to Jachin and Boaz, the pillars of the Temple of Solomon. They are an expression of justice and benevolence, and thus the cornerstones of humanity.

Rose: the three roses, which the Freemasons also put onto the graves of their deceased, stand for love, loyalty, and gratitude, or love, light, and life.

Rough ashlar: the symbol of imperfection and thus of the Entered Apprentice. It characterizes the stage of self-awareness.

Sun and moon: seen as signs of God's power, eternity, omnipresence, and goodness.

Temple: symbol of the most sacred building work. It stands for the path to self-perfection ("inner temple") as well as for the ideal of humanity co-existing in peace ("temple of humanity").

Triangle: symbolizes the idea that all the secrets of the universe can be uncovered through the science of numbers. The symbol thus corresponds to the Master Mason degree and refers to the stage of self-improvement.

A SOCIETY WITH SECRETS

The Freemasons' separation from, and secretiveness toward, non-Masons have often resulted in public suspicion of the lodges. The rules and rituals of the fraternity are now widely known, but their "secrets" are incomprehensible to outsiders.

Vow of Secrecy

The Freemasons see themselves not as a secret society, but as a "society with secrets." All newly admitted brothers pledge themselves, on entering the lodge, to "keep secret the rituals and internal affairs of Freemasonry and not to speak of them to anyone."

Closed doors and darkened windows. The temple work of the Freemasons takes place behind closed doors. Secrecy is the paramount precept.

Time and again over the centuries, this vow, also referred to as the "arcane discipline," has contributed to the fraternity being suspected of having secret intentions and aims, even of being a worldwide conspiracy. On the other hand, the structures, rules and rituals of Freemasonry are well known. The only things that are kept secret are the brothers' agreed signs of recognition and the details of the rituals. Nonetheless, people often talk about the "secrets" of the Freemasons.

The Secret of the Rituals

There are no grounds for believing that Freemasonry has secret leaders or secret knowledge and magic formulae, or that it pursues secret aims. Nor does it keep anything secret to the detriment of others. Its secrets do not consist of any gruesome rituals, black masses, or blood sacrifices, as has been implied. The secrets of Freemasonry consist of knowledge that is only accessible to the initiated, and which is substantially shrouded in symbols and rituals. They lie in the essence of mystic rituals that are difficult to express in words. The highly symbolic content of these acts, as well as the spiritual experiences gathered by the individual during the ritual, are barely comprehensible to the outsider. Even someone who knows about all of the possible meanings of the symbols and is familiar with the exact sequence of the Masonic rituals will learn nothing more than the rules of the game. Rituals are spiritual acts that can only be completely understood by someone who has experienced and lived through them.

Discretion Establishes Trust

There are further grounds for the Freemasons' arcane discipline: Secrecy is the most important requirement for trust between the brothers.

Johann Wolfgang von Goethe (1749–1832), himself an active Freemason, expressed it as follows in his lodge poem *Verschwiegenheit* ("Secrecy"): "No-one should and will see / what we have confided in each other; / for on

The annual international meetings of Freemasons and a few selected lodge functions are the only events open to the public. Only in a few countries do the Freemasons actively participate in social life as a group.

silence and trust / is the Temple built!" People can only reveal intimate things about themselves if they do not have to worry that tomorrow their neighbors will already have found out about it.

There is a further reason why the meetings of Masons are not open to non-Masons: Ritual work in a group can succeed only if it is not disturbed by the "profane," who do not understand the essence of what is taking place and are therefore unable to understand its impact. Since their rituals sometimes seem strange to non-initiates, the fraternity seeks to escape the scorn and ridicule of outsiders by setting itself apart.

Declaration of the Grand Lodge

In response to the accusation that the Freemasons were a secret society, the United Grand Lodges of Germany declared in June 1980: "The citizen justifiably wants to know who is influencing the way in which the state and society are organized and what their intentions are. Genuine secret societies conceal everything that might point to their existence [. . .]. The Freemasons' lodges are quite different: They are organized in accordance with civil law, their statutes can be inspected in the register of associations, as can their organizational structure and the names of those who hold office; their domiciles are meeting places."

The Organization
of the Freemasons

Since the eighteenth century, all lodges recognized by the "mother" Grand Lodge of All England as being "regular" have been recorded in the List of Regular Masonic Lodges.

THE LODGE

The organizational structure of Freemasonry has a clear hierarchy: The individual lodges come under the provincial lodges, which in turn fall under the jurisdiction of the Grand Lodge and its Grand Master. In each lodge, the Worshipful Master presides over the Master Masons, Fellow Crafts, and Entered Apprentices of the fraternity.

Grand Lodges and Individual Lodges

Freemasonry is organized into lodges and Grand Lodges. Lodge (*loge* in French) means "hut" or "arbor." In Freemasonry the term signifies three things: The fraternity itself, its central meeting place (also called the lodge temple), and finally its ritual activities. Some fraternities still refer to themselves today as guilds, to keep alive the memory of the medieval origins of organized Freemasonry. Lodges that have retained the original division into the three degrees of Entered Apprentice, Fellow Craft, and Master Mason are called "Craft lodges" or "blue lodges."

As well as these, there are also the so-called "red lodges," which have considerably more degrees, the "high degrees." Most lodges today are organized as associations and entered in the register of associations. The number of Masonic lodges worldwide is estimated at around 40,000–45,000. As there is no global Masonic organization, more precise figures are not known. In order to found a lodge, a minimum of nine men is

required, of whom seven must be Master Masons.
A lodge can only be active when at least seven persons
are present, three of whom must be Master Masons.

The Lodge System

Each individual lodge is subordinate to a Grand Lodge.
These represent the individual lodges affiliated to them
in public, supervise their work and their adherence to
Masonic principles, and can dissolve them in cases of
conflict. They provide individual lodges with suggestions
for charitable and cultural activities, and also maintain
contact with other Grand Lodges domestically and
abroad. A lodge may apply to become affiliated to a
Grand Lodge. This takes place through a process known
as "consecration," which is the preserve of the respective
Grand Master of the Grand Lodge, leading to the
applicant lodge being entered in its membership list.
It is this entry that makes the lodge a "regular" lodge.
Linking the Grand Lodges and the individual lodges are
the district or provincial lodges, whose officers are
elected directly by the fraternities based in their
particular district. Besides these, there are also research
lodges, which study the past and present of
Freemasonry. The oldest of these research lodges was
founded in London in 1844.

The Work of the Lodges

Most lodges meet once a week. Each lodge is obliged by
its Grand Lodge to perform a specified number of ritual
activities, during the course of which new members are
admitted to the lodge as Entered Apprentices, and
brothers can attain their next Masonic degree. This
"temple work" is generally followed by a communal
meal at which participants sit down at the "white table."
In addition to their ritual gatherings, lodges commonly
also host lecture evenings, debates, and charity balls.

The "Worshipful Master" heads the hierarchy of each lodge. He must
conduct his life in such a way that he serves as a shining example to all
his brother Masons.

The "Worshipful Master"

Each lodge has a strictly hierarchical structure. In
order to create a leadership, the lodge members
elect a committee of officers for a specified period
of time. At its head is the "Worshipful Master." He
must be suitable, in terms of the way he conducts
himself, to serve as a role model to all the brethren.
The Worshipful Master is supported by further
officers: Two Wardens, the Master Elect, the Orator,
the Secretary, and the Treasurer. The committee
may sometimes also be extended to include a
director of ceremonies, the so-called Marshal, and
a Librarian. Each of these roles has very specific
tasks assigned to it.

THE INTERNATIONAL SYSTEM OF LODGES

In Freemasonry, there is no international leadership hierarchy above the national Grand Lodges. All lodges function largely autonomously. The main differences between them lie in the question of belief in a supreme being and the number of Masonic degrees. In addition to "regular" Freemasonry, there are also "irregular" fraternities, which are not recognized by the English Mother Lodge (*see below*).

The London Freemasons' Hall is one of the most historically significant sites in international Freemasonry: It was here that the reunification of the two previously estranged English Grand Lodges took place in 1813.

A Chain of Brothers Encircling the World

There is no international organization or world authority in Freemasonry. The Grand Lodges and lodges in each country are organized autonomously. In Germany, the *Bruderschaft der deutschen Freimaurer* ("Fraternity of German Freemasons") is the umbrella organization for five Grand Lodges. The bonds linking the regular Grand Lodges all over the world, which number well over one hundred, are cemented by the fundamental principles of Freemasonry and, above all, its rituals and symbols. The Grand Lodges mutually recognize one another and their members have reciprocal visiting rights. These are the pillars on which the Freemasons' "chain of brothers encircling the world" is based.

A Religious Factional Dispute

Throughout the history of Freemasonry, there have been innumerable schisms resulting in particular associations, systems, and groupings. However, not all of these are recognized as Freemasonic associations. Only those fraternities that are officially accepted by the Grand Lodge of England, the Mother Lodge of Freemasonry, are deemed to be "regular" Grand Lodges. The founding of each lodge requires the warrant of a regular Grand Lodge.

During the course of its history, three major directions of Freemasonry have emerged with regard to belief in a divine "Great Architect of the Universe." While most lodges insist on the avowal of a belief in a higher divine being—an avowal, however, that is so general that it

Coats of arms have always played an important role for craft guilds as a way of promoting the identification of members with their own guilds. The Freemasons' lodges have also taken up this tradition.

Arthur William Patrick Albert (1850–1942), Duke of Connaught and son of Queen Victoria, was, like many members of the English royal family, a member of a Freemasons' lodge.

accepts adherents of all religions—a minority of lodges insist on Christian doctrine. Those fraternities that also admit members who do not believe in any kind of deity (*see p34*) are not officially recognized and are therefore deemed irregular. Today, lodges are referred to as "Christian" or "humanitarian," depending on whether they take a more Christian or a more secular approach.

Regular and Irregular

Lodges that accept women or breach other Masonic principles are also deemed to be irregular. These principles, the so-called "landmarks," include, for example, the precept of secrecy and the use of symbols. The "Basic Principles," first issued in 1929 and last revised in 1989, currently form the main basis for differentiating between regular and irregular Freemasonry.

Moderns and Antients

As early as 1751, 34 years after the founding of the Grand Lodge of England, the first split occurred in organized Freemasonry. Under the leadership of the writer Laurence Dermott (1720–91), the Christian-oriented "Antients" (The Antient Grand Lodge of England) seceded from the Grand Lodge of England, the "Moderns." While the Moderns were heavily dependent on members of noble birth, the Antients' members were considerably more bourgeois. An additional fourth degree, the "Royal Arch," was at the core of the Antients' doctrinal system.

Although the English Grand Lodges were reunited in a grand ceremony at Freemasons' Hall in London in 1813, becoming the United Grand Lodge of England, the Royal Arch system is still widespread today in the US and in France as well as being part of the York Rite system of Masonic degrees (*see p 52*).

THE DEGREES

Freemasonic teachings are divided into so-called degrees. Initiation processes lead from one degree to the next.

The Blue Degrees

In the original Freemasonry of the seventeenth century there were only two degrees: Entered Apprentice and Fellow Craft. However, in around 1730 this developed into the three-stage system of regular Freemasonry, with the Master Mason degree being incorporated into the system. This ritual division into three harks back to the ancient church masons' guilds and the craft traditions: It is the Master Mason who is entrusted with the leadership and planning of the project, and is responsible for the work carried out by the journeymen or Fellow Crafts. The training stage is symbolized by the Entered Apprentice degree. These three Masonic degrees, through which the brothers are meant to progress from "rough" stone to "hewn" stone, encompass the entire content of Masonic teachings.

Guthrie, Oklahoma, is home to the Temple of the Scottish Rite of Freemasonry. This Rite, with its 33 degrees, is the most well-known and widespread system of high-degree Freemasonry.

An Initiation for Each Degree

Each new Freemason enters the first degree through a ritual initiation. At the conclusion of the ceremony, the seeker makes his vow before an altar adorned with the three "great lights"—holy book, square, and compasses. He does this kneeling and blindfold. His right foot touches the square, his left hand guides the compasses to his breast, and his right hand rests on the holy book.

An Entered Apprentice's admission to the Fellow Craft degree marks the completion of his apprenticeship. The initiation rituals are similar to those for the Entered Apprentice degree: The Entered Apprentice must answer several questions, withdraw into the dark chamber and finally undertake a ritual journey in which he is symbolically confronted with several temptations. Most Freemasons remain for at least a year in the Entered Apprentice and Fellow Craft grades respectively.

For the test to become a Master Mason, the Fellow Craft must ritually endure the death of Hiram (*see box on p 12*), in order to be awakened to new life by the Master Mason's word. Once he has progressed to Master Mason, he can then undertake official duties within the lodge.

High-Degree Freemasonry

The three degrees of the Craft lodges comprise the entire tradition of Freemasonry. Nonetheless, during the eighteenth century the so-called "high-degree systems" emerged alongside the Craft degrees. These systems see themselves as a "university of Freemasonry": A "continuation," "perfection," or "selection."

The high-degrees, referred to as "red," do not differ fundamentally from "blue" Freemasonry, rather they enlarge upon the teachings of the Apprentice, Fellow Craft, and Master Mason degrees.

The number of degrees and their significance depend on the rite concerned. Differentiations are made between the "York Rite," "Royal Arch Rite," "French Rite," "Swedish Rite," and the "Ancient and Accepted Scottish Rite." The latter, the most well-known of all the high-degree systems, which emerged in around 1800, has 33 degrees which are conferred by different controlling bodies. Many of them incorporate traditions from the Order of the Templars (*see pp 16–17*).

The three degrees of traditional "blue Freemasonry" are derived directly from the hierarchy that has existed in the Craft since time immemorial. There were apprentices, journeymen, and master masons on the very first construction sites on earth.

The 33 Degrees of the Ancient and Accepted Scottish Rite

1. Entered Apprentice
2. Fellow Craft
3. Master Mason
4. Master Traveler
5. Perfect Master
6. Intimate Secretary
7. Provost and Judge
8. Intendant of the Building
9. Elu of the Nine
10. Elu of the Fifteen
11. Sublime Master Elected
12. Grand Master Architect
13. Master of the Ninth Arch
14. Grand Elect Mason
15. Knight of the Sword
16. Prince of Jerusalem
17. Knight of the East and West
18. Knight Rose Croix
19. Grand Pontiff
20. Grand Master of all Symbolic Lodges
21. Prussian Knight
22. Prince of Libanus
23. Chief of the Tabernacle
24. Prince of the Tabernacle
25. Knight of the Brazen Serpent
26. Prince of Mercy
27. Knight Commander of the Temple
28. Knight of the Sun
29. Knight of St. Andrew of Scotland
30. Knight Kadosh
31. Inspector Inquisitor
32. Sublime Prince of the Royal Secret
33. Sovereign Grand Inspector General

The master smith initiates his apprentice into the art of the craft. As in a craftsman's workshop, Master Masons in Masonic lodges are responsible for instructing Entered Apprentices.

THE HIGH-DEGREE SYSTEMS

On many occasions during the history of Freemasonry, groups have seceded from traditional Craft Freemasonry; these groupings have often achieved a high level of influence and gained many lodges for their systems. Most of these divisions operate high-degree systems, which can have up to 90 levels.

The Ancient and Accepted Scottish Rite

In the eighteenth century, many Freemasons felt the need to broaden and build on the basic teachings of the first three degrees. In their search for spiritual sources,

they came across traditional Scottish Freemasonry, and from this they developed the Masonic high degrees. The lodges of the most important of these systems, the "Ancient and Accepted Scottish Rite," are affiliated to the Supreme Council of Grand Inspector Generals, founded in Charleston, South Carolina, in 1801. Its power is roughly equivalent to that of the United Grand Lodge of England.

The 30 degrees that are added to the three blue degrees are further subdivided into "red" (4th to 18th degrees), "black" (19th to 30th degrees), and "white" (31st to 33rd degrees). However, only seven of these degrees play a practical role, in that promotion of Freemasons to them involves special initiation

Each degree has its own symbol: The high-degree systems of the Scottish and York Rites are almost unintelligible to the uninitiated.

ceremonies. These are contained in the teachings of the "white" degrees, as well as the fourth, ninth, and eighteenth degrees.

The Rectified Scottish Rite

Unlike the Ancient and Accepted Scottish Rite, this "rectified" Masonic association has only six degrees. The highest of these degrees is the "Knight Beneficent of the Holy City," in memory of the Knights Templar. This rite, which has a very spiritual character with pronounced Christian traits, is most common today in Switzerland, Belgium, and France.

The York Rite

The York Rite is a group of Masonic rituals, some of them very old, which are found principally today in the US and Canada. Alongside the three Craft degrees, this system has four further so-called capitular degrees as well as three cryptic degrees, the degree of Super Excellent Master being the highest of these. One of the most important bodies in the York Rite is the Christian Masonic Order of the Knights Templar. The rituals of this fraternity, founded in 1769 in Boston, are most

common in the US, England, and Ireland, and are closely associated with the traditions of the Templars and the Crusaders.

The Swedish Rite

The Swedish Rite, also called the Swedenborg Rite, was founded in around 1776 by the Benedictine monk, Antoine Joseph Pernetty (1716–96). It draws in particular on the Christian gospels, medieval mysticism, and the teachings of the Swedish naturalist and spiritualist Emanuel Swedenborg (1688–1772). The Swedish Rite is characterized by numerous esoteric and occult elements, and depending on the variant it has nine, ten, or eleven different degrees. This rite gained a foothold in the US and Canada during the second half of the nineteenth century, but it has been greatly altered, so the current form no longer has much in common with the original.

The teachings of the Swedish researcher and mystic Emanuel Swedenborg form the framework of the Swedish Rite, a strongly esoteric branch of Freemasonry.

How do you Become a Freemason?

Anyone who wants to become a Freemason must fulfill a whole range of criteria; ultimately it is the lodge brethren who decide, voting with black and white balls, whether the "seeker" should be admitted.

Free-Born and of Good Report

According to James Anderson's *Book of Constitutions* of 1723, which is still seen as the constitution of Freemasons, all "Men, Free-born…of good report" could be admitted to a lodge. "Free" here means, above all, an inner freedom, the freedom to make important, life-affecting decisions autonomously. However, many lodges also make the absence of specific psychological dependencies—ranging from a passion for gambling to drug addiction—a prerequisite for admittance. In addition, the person seeking admittance, known in Masonic language as the "seeker," should have a certain level of financial security, so that he is able to afford to undertake the tasks associated with the work of the lodge and to procure the typical Masonic clothing (apron, gloves, lodge emblem). For candidates on low incomes, however, these costs can be waived or deferred

Admission, Transfer, and Resignation

Freemasons see acceptance into a lodge as the forging of a lifetime bond. The elaborate and time-consuming admission procedure therefore also serves the purpose of preventing casual admissions. Notwithstanding this, however, resignations are readily possible and are generally referred to as "honorable demits." Transferring to a different lodge is also commonplace.

Even among the Freemasons, the title of Master Mason is not easy to attain. The road to becoming a Worshipful Grand Master is long and paved with numerous trials.

in specific cases. The "good report" does not have to be validated by a police certificate of good conduct, but the candidate should name a referee who can provide information about him. It is also important that the seeker should, in line with the old charges, be honest, honorable, and free from racial, religious or political prejudice. He must declare his willingness to put himself to the test and to change. He must not be a member of any organization hostile to the Freemasons. It is a matter of principle that young men under the age of majority cannot enter the fraternity, but in many lodges candidates must have completed their 21st year.

The Seeker Must Declare Himself

The admission criteria vary, although not in substance, from lodge to lodge. Most new Freemasons come to a lodge through the recommendation of a brother. Most lodges reject advertising, on the grounds that the moral conduct of individual Freemasons should speak for itself, and thus also for the fraternity. One exception is the French *Grand Orient*, not recognized by the English Grand Lodge, which puts out public radio broadcasts.

In general, those who approach a lodge wishing to be admitted are asked to submit a written application including a CV. Seekers are generally expected to attend guest evenings, which take place at regular intervals, for at least six months. At these he will get to know the lodge brothers. He will be asked to give comprehensive and truthful information about his reasons for wanting to join the lodge. During this time, the candidate must find one or two sponsors who will support him during his years as an Entered Apprentice and, subsequently, as a Fellow Craft.

Anyone wearing the traditional ceremonial costume at a public Freemasonic event usually has many years in a fraternity already behind him.

Black Balls Mean Rejection

In front of the lodge's admissions committee, the candidate will once more be asked about his desire to become a Freemason. When the sponsors have been found and the committee has expressed a positive recommendation, the balloting takes place. In an elective, or ostracizational, method that dates back to ancient Greece, and from which we take the term "blackball", the brothers vote on the acceptance by means of black and white balls. White means yes, black means no. If the result is "clear in the south," that is, all the balls are white, there is nothing further to prevent the seeker's initiation. If too many black balls are cast in the secret ballot, he is deemed to have been rejected.

Seton Challon (center of photo) Grand Mistress of a women's Freemasonry lodge, is one of the pioneers of female Freemasonry. However, women-only lodges are still not officially recognized.

THE ISSUE OF WOMEN

Freemasonry is a men's organization. While lodges that admit women have been accepted for over 250 years, they are not officially recognized.

Open Hearts, Closed Lodges

Women are excluded from membership of a regular Freemasonic lodge. This stems from the fact that at the time Freemasonry came into being there were no female stonemasons, and it is from the medieval church masons' guilds that Freemasonry evolved.

As early as 1723, in the *Book of Constitutions*, Freemasonry explicitly bans women from admission to the fraternities. A text on the Freemasons' image of themselves, printed in *Der Teutsche Merkur* ("The German Mercury") in 1785, states unequivocally, "The hearts of Freemasons are open to women, but their

Women are not People

There is historical evidence to show that before the official beginnings of Freemasonry, in isolated instances in England and in France, women were being initiated into the rites of Freemasonic associations. That these were indeed isolated cases was principally due to the fact that in the eighteenth century women had far fewer rights than men and were often not regarded as equal to men. Thus the English philosopher John Stuart Mill (1806–73) deplored the fact that "the wife is the actual bond-servant of her husband...as far as legal obligation goes." The saying common at that time, "*Gallina non est avis, uxor non est homo*" ("A hen is not a bird, a woman is not a person") explains the position in a nutshell.

lodges are closed to them." This situation has not fundamentally changed since then.

The "Basic Principles" of Freemasonry published in 1929 by the English Grand Lodge also stress that regular lodges may not admit women. Many lodges fear even today that their brethren would be "distracted" from their ritual temple work by women.

Initially Adopted, then Independent: The Mixed Lodges

The "issue of women" has been hotly debated in Freemasonry ever since the decision of the English Freemasons' Grand Lodge not to admit women. In the meantime, three types of lodge in which women can participate have come into being, but none of these have been recognized as regular lodges. As early as the middle of the eighteenth century, there were "adoption lodges," in which men and women worked Masonic rituals together. These societies, however, were not recognized either independently or officially, but were attached to existing male lodges and controlled by them. Such mixed lodges originated principally in France; the French Queen Marie Antoinette (1755–93), for example, belonged to such a lodge.

At the end of the nineteenth century, the first independent "mixed" lodges appeared, also in France. In 1882, the famous French feminist Maria Deraismes (1828–94) was admitted to the Paris *Les Libres Penseurs* ("Free Thinkers") lodge, which subsequently lost its recognition. Deraismes founded the first mixed lodge, *Le Droit Humain* ("The Human Right") 11 years later, to which 16 other women were also initially admitted. *Le Droit Humain* soon converted into a Grand Lodge, and further mixed Grand Lodges were founded over the following decades, initially in Europe, then in India, the US, South America, and Oceania. Today, there are daughter lodges of *Le Droit Humain* in more than 60 countries, with an estimated 400,000 members.

Women-Only Lodges

Then at the beginning of the twentieth century, the first women-only lodges began to appear, first in England and the US, but they were likewise not recognized as regular. Later, this type of lodge also emerged in France, Spain, Belgium, and Switzerland. In Germany, the women's lodge *Zur Humanität* ("For Humanity") was founded in 1949 and converted to a Grand Lodge in 1982. This sorority, which has since been renamed the *Frauen-Großloge von Deutschland* ("Women's Grand Lodge of Germany"), now has 15 daughter lodges in German cities. Today women-only lodges are also to be found in numerous South American countries.

The French Queen Marie Antoinette is probably the most prominent female Freemason of the eighteenth century. She belonged to a mixed lodge that had been "adopted" by a male fraternity.

At a meeting of female Freemasons in London in 1937, the "sisters" announced their demand to be granted equal recognition within the international system of Freemasonry.

The History of
Freemasonry

THE CHURCH AND FREEMASONRY

The history of Freemasonry is one of growth and expansion, but also of persecution, suppression, and bloodshed. Since the beginnings of organized Freemasonry, the fraternity has been the subject of suspicion and persecution by the Catholic Church. For over 230 years, the Vatican forbade believers to join a lodge and threatened Catholic Freemasons with excommunication.

The Mark of Evil

Since the eighteenth century, there has been a deep, almost unbridgeable chasm between the Catholic Church and Freemasonry. From the beginning, the Church had suspected the Freemasons of practicing

Pope Pius VII, who led the Catholic Church from 1800–23, was one of the sharpest critics of Freemasons' lodges. In 1814, he accused the fraternities of being a threat to state security.

blasphemy and conducting orgies in which they allegedly indulged in drunkenness and sexual acts with minors. That the Freemasons' associations had aroused such strong suspicion is apparent in a papal bull issued by Pope Clement XII on April 28, 1738, condemning the brotherhood: "A righteous and wise man cannot join these societies without tarnishing himself with the mark of perversion and evil." It was the Freemasons' strict maintenance of secrecy, in particular, which aroused the Church's distrust. The papal edict stated, "If they were not doing evil they would not have so great a hatred of the light." It prohibited believers from joining a lodge. Those who flouted this ban were threatened with excommunication—banishment from the Church. The papal bull led to the banning of Masonic fraternities in Spain, Portugal, and Poland. The main thorn in the flesh of the Catholic Church was the fact that the Freemasons accepted people of all religions and did not place any one denomination above any other. However, even the threat of banishment from the Church could not prevent many clergymen—including prelates and bishops—from becoming Freemasons.

Freemasonry and the Protestant Church

The relationship between the Protestant Church and Freemasonry has always been less fraught than relations between the lodges and the Vatican. More than one Masonic Grand Master has worn the cassock of a Protestant clergyman.

The Church itself repeatedly posed the question of whether a Christian could be a Freemason, but never answered with an unequivocal "no." This ambivalence centered on the conviction that Masonic humanity should not be equated with that of the New Testament, which alone had its source in the grace of the Christian God.

For more than 200 years, the Vatican aggressively denounced Freemasonry. Governments in southern European countries, in particular, used the Catholic hostility toward Freemasons to legitimize ruthless action against the lodges.

Freemasonry as the Work of the Devil

Throughout the nineteenth century, too, Freemasons and the Church were still openly at war with one another, with the clergy persistently taking the role of the aggressor. Many Christian-oriented lodges, on the other hand, repeatedly emphasized their "sincere devotion to the Holy Christian religion," partly as an attempt to lessen the vehemence of attacks by the Church. These attempts at appeasement bore little fruit: In 1814, Pope Pius VII denounced the brotherhood as a threat to the security of the state. 50 years later, Pope Pius IX described Freemasonry as the "synagogue of Satan," attacking the idea that reason should be put above faith. His successor, Leo XIII, condemned the fraternity as the very "work of the Devil" which was said to involve a "deadly hatred of the Church" and adjured all Catholic bishops to eradicate this "unclean thing."

Conciliation with "A Grave Sin"

These attacks continued until well into the twentieth century. From 1968, the Catholic Church under Pope Paul VI entered into a cautious dialog with the Masonic lodges, although this only led to a limited conciliation. An official Commission in 1970 declared that "the papal bulls relating to Freemasonry are now of only historical importance." A mere 11 years later, however, the Vatican confirmed that members of a Freemasonic society should continue to be excluded from the Church. The threat of "automatic" exclusion was withdrawn shortly afterwards, but in truth, the relationship between the Catholic Church and Freemasonry is still strained today.

For example, the German Cardinal Joseph Ratzinger, who as Pope Benedict XVI has led the Catholic Church since April 2005, has declared that it is "a grave sin" to be a member of a lodge.

Many Freemasons took an active part in the French Revolution, although the Masonic rules forbid any involvement by lodges in politics. However, the ideals of the Enlightenment matched the Freemasons' ethics.

THE FREEMASONS: STATE AND POLITICS

Freemasonry sees itself as apolitical and loyal to the state. Nonetheless, Freemasons have time and again been in the vanguard of social upheavals directed against the ruling system of government.

Loyalty to the State

The relationship between Freemasonry and the state was, particularly in the eighteenth century, extremely ambivalent—there was a deep divide between theory and practice. As early as 1723, James Anderson's *Book of Constitutions*, obligated the fraternities to be loyal to the state's "supremacy," and renounced any form of rebellion against the power of the state. In these "Old Charges" it is written, "A Mason is a peaceable Subject to the Civil Powers, wherever he resides or works, and is never to be concern'd in Plots and Conspiracies against the Peace and Welfare of the Nation." The Freemasons have always seen themselves, in almost all countries, as an apolitical organization that does not interfere in the politics of the day. Although individual lodge brethren are permitted to engage in politics, arguments about party political issues have always been proscribed by Freemasonry. According to the "Old Charges," the Mason should strive in: "Avoiding…doing or saying anything offensive, or that may forbid an easy and free Conversation for that would blast our Harmony, and defeat our laudable Purposes. Therefore no private Piques or Quarrels must be brought within the Door of the Lodge, far less any Quarrels about Religion, or Nations, or State-Policy, we being . . . of all Nations, Tongues, Kindreds, and Languages, and resolved against all politics as what never yet conduced to the welfare of the Lodge, nor ever will."

Enlightenment Ideals

In practice, however, things look different. Even where lodges stand aloof from any kind of party politics, this does not prevent social and political developments and goals being welcomed by Freemasons. These include, first and foremost, the separation of State and Church, the establishment of secular public schools, the internationalization of politics in the direction of world citizenship, and the enforcement of democratic principles. The inner structure of the lodges has from the outset been characterized by the principle of self-organization by brethren of equal status. At the time of the formation of the first official lodges, they were thus a precursor of the modern democratic system.

Particularly in the eighteenth century, the Freemasonic virtues of equality and fraternity were in open opposition to the policies of the ruling royal houses. By contrast, the ideas of the Enlightenment that started in France and ultimately culminated in bourgeois revolutions in half of Europe, came fairly close to the ideals espoused by the Freemasons. A similar conflict emerged in the British colonies in North America. Here, the settlers were demanding to be freed from the yoke of the authoritarian British colonial administration. In both cases, many members of the Freemasons' lodges, which had sworn allegiance to the state, were eventually to be found in the vanguard of the political upheavals directed against the state's authority. They played a decisive part in the French Revolution and in the War of Independence in North America. Even today, most French and American lodges are more politically oriented than fraternities in other countries.

Persecuted by the State

Freemasons have been repeatedly persecuted and banned by state authorities. As a result, they have often been forced—for the sake of their own survival—into opposing these ruling powers. Dictators on both the Left and the Right have been particularly intolerant of Freemasons, firstly because of their democratic basic principles, and secondly because it was difficult for the state to exert any influence over them. Fraternities have also been banned by fundamentalist religious governments.

Since the French Revolution, French Freemasons have been more heavily involved in political conflicts than their lodge brothers in other countries. Here, Freemasons are demonstrating in Paris for a better education system.

THE CULTURE OF THE FREEMASONS

Freemasons have influenced culture in many ways, not only with their spirit of Enlightenment, but also with numerous works by famous artists that have Freemasonic themes at their core.

The Culture of Perfection

The Freemasons' understanding of the purpose of culture is first and foremost that it should ennoble and perfect a person; culture should show the individual a way in which he can structure his life meaningfully. In this way, the shaping of a man's life becomes a personal work of art. The Freemason should create his work like a master mason, but as a master of the art of living.

The cultural significance of Freemasonry lies primarily in its tolerant way of uniting as many creeds and socio-political viewpoints as possible into one system. In doing so, it bridges understanding and experience.

The Magic Flute and *Nathan the Wise*

The symbols and rituals guiding this experience have been cultivated and enlarged upon in numerous speeches, songs, poems, and novels by distinguished Masonic musicians, composers, and writers. Freemasonry has an extensive literature about its teachings, its history, and its customs; it has also created its own treasury of songs. Freemasonic chants and drinking songs were composed from the early

The Magic Flute is not only one of Wolfgang Amadeus Mozart's most famous operas, but also a parable of Freemasonry. Tamino (at the center of the photo) personifies the seeker, who must undergo numerous ordeals.

More than any other, *The Magic Flute* is seen as a Masonic work. Mozart based some of the scenes directly on the lodges' initiation rituals.

Gotthold Ephraim Lessing was another famous Freemason. Unmistakably Masonic themes are to be found in *Nathan the Wise* and in some of his other theatrical works.

eighteenth century onward, and were later compiled in songbooks. The greatest treasure of Freemasonic music was created by Wolfgang Amadeus Mozart (1756–91) in his opera *The Magic Flute*; this famous Freemason also composed a series of solo songs and cantatas for his lodge.

The most important Freemasonic drama is considered to be the play *Nathan the Wise* by Gotthold Ephraim Lessing (1729–81). Its "ring parable" ranks as a teaching play for Freemasons all over the world. Freemasonic themes also occur repeatedly in the works of the

philosopher Johann Gottlieb Fichte (1762–1814) and of the writers Rudyard Kipling (1865–1935), and Christoph Martin Wieland (1733–1813).

A Center for Artists: The *Zur wahren Eintracht* Lodge

More than anything else, however, Freemasonry in the eighteenth century, with its ethics based on the principles of equality, tolerance, and fraternity, characterized the intellectual culture of the time and helped to prepare the ground for the European Age of Enlightenment. Many lodges that had eminent and erudite members became centers of philosophy and culture, for example the Parisian lodge *Les Neuf Sœurs* ("The Nine Sisters"), which was also described as a philosophers' lodge, and the Viennese lodge *Zur wahren Eintracht* ("True Harmony"). This lodge, founded in 1781, took on the character of a Freemasonic academy.

Almost all Viennese writers, musicians, and scientists of distinction became members of the fraternity. At their head was the natural scientist and satirist Ignaz von Born (1742–91), one of the most scintillating personalities of the reign of Joseph II.

Mozart's *Magic Flute*

Mozart's most famous opera is a parable of Freemasonry. It describes the path of the seeker toward the light, personified by Tamino, who must undergo numerous (ostensibly Masonic) ordeals. Some scenes seem to have been taken directly from the initiation rituals of a lodge. The character of the wise Sarastro personifies the ideal Freemasonic image of humanity, and it is thought that Mozart based him on the lodge Master Ignaz von Born, whom he revered.

The storming of the Bastille marked the zenith of the French Revolution. Many Freemasons joined the rebels and took part in the storming of the French state prison.

IN THE SPIRIT OF THE ENLIGHTENMENT

The history of European Freemasonry in the second half of the eighteenth century is very closely linked to the social and political developments of the time.

Growth and Fragmentation

In England, the development of lodges was marked by steady growth, but also by the fragmentation of the system. The United Grand Lodge of England, founded in 1717, already had 109 lodges under its aegis by 1732, and this figure had risen to more than 400 by 1813. This growth coincided with the creation of the Freemasonic high-degree system in 1740 together with the inception of numerous new Masonic teachings that conflicted with the principles of the English Grand Lodge. To differentiate themselves from the latter, further Grand Lodge systems were set up. The Antient Grand Lodge of England, founded in 1751, was particularly popular. By

1781, 200 lodges already belonged to the Antients. In other European countries, too, growth and fragmentation of the lodges went hand-in-hand. In Germany, this fragmentation was exacerbated by the break-up of the country into numerous small states. The wide variety of Freemasonic lodges in turn organized themselves under a large number of newly founded Grand Lodges.

Bans and Persecution

The Catholic Church not only took action against the lodges through papal decrees, but also brought its influence to bear on governments. This helped to bring about numerous bans, and between 1731 and 1739 alone, fraternities were closed down in Italy, Switzerland, Germany, Holland, Poland, and Sweden. The action taken against Freemasons by the Catholic was most systematic in Spain and Portugal.

Enlightenment and Revolution

In the anti-progressive atmosphere of countries ruled by royal and princely families, Freemasonry became a new form of protest against social and political injustices. The lodges removed differences of status in their ranks: Here there were no subordinates, just brothers on an equal footing. In this way, the Freemasonic lodges attracted many personalities who were advocating a more humane world. They represented the view that every man had a basic right to freedom and education, and that reason was the measure of all things. It was possible for these fundamental ideas of the Enlightenment to unfold freely in the isolation of the Freemasons' lodges.

This trend was particularly pronounced in France: In the face of the abuses of the absolute monarchy under Louis XV (1715–74) and his successor Louis XVI (1774–92), the first Freemasonic circles of noblemen formed which were opposed to the Crown. In 1737, Freemasonry was banned, and the persecution of those lodges that refused to disband began.

At the same time, the spirit of the Enlightenment was spreading ever wider. Important French figures of the Enlightenment, in particular artists and scientists, joined forces with the Freemasons. Voltaire (1694–1778), probably the movement's most important thinker, joined a lodge shortly before his death. The spirit of the Enlightenment eventually led to the French Revolution.

When, in 1789, large sections of the French people rose up against Louis XVI and stormed the Paris state prison, the Bastille, there were many Freemasons among the rebels.

The lodges themselves, however, did not take part in the uprisings, as removing a government by force was contrary to Freemasonic principles. Nonetheless, the revolutionary events led to the temporary decline of French Freemasonry—the fraternities were banned, and numerous Freemasons executed. It was not until 1793 that some lodges were able to reestablish themselves.

The philosopher Voltaire is seen as one of the founding fathers of the French Enlightenment. Shortly before his death he became a Freemason, like many other progressive French thinkers.

Large sections of the French populace, along with many Freemasons who were opposed to the Crown, rose up against the abuses of the absolute monarchy under Louis XVI.

FREEMASONS IN THE AMERICAN INDEPENDENCE MOVEMENT

No other political development has been as closely linked with Freemasonry as the emergence of the US. Freemasons played a decisive role in the War of Independence against the British colonial rulers, as well as in the later founding of the nation.

New York's Statue of Liberty— a Freemasonic Creation

The Statue of Liberty is a Freemasonic creation. The creator of the 150 ft (46 meters) statue was the French sculptor Frédéric-Auguste Bartholdi (1834–1904), who had been admitted to the Parisian Alsace-Lorraine lodge in 1874. The Freemason Gustave Eiffel (1832–1923), the designer of the Eiffel Tower, produced the huge iron skeleton that supports the copper statue from within. French Freemasons collected the money to pay for the statue, while American lodge brothers raised the cost of the pedestal, which is over 165 ft (50 meters) high. Finally, the foundation stone for "Miss Liberty," completed in 1886, was laid by the Grand Lodge of New York.

The Foundation of Independence

In the middle of the eighteenth century, the Freemasonic fraternity in the British colonies of North America comprised around 6,000 men. For the most part, they were organized into small lodges, which received their warrants primarily from the English Grand Lodges, or in some cases from the Scottish ones. Besides the United Grand Lodge of England (Moderns), the Antient Grand Lodge of England, which seceded from it in 1751, soon also started to issue foundation charters. The lodges of the Moderns principally admitted royal governors, high-ranking officers, and officials, the majority of whom did not want to make the break from England. In the Antients' lodges, on the other hand, tradesmen and other proponents of independence for the North American colonies were generally in the majority.

Freemasons as the Driving Force Behind the Movement

The ideas of equality and fraternity, and of human rights and democracy without social boundaries and state suppression fell on fertile ground in the New World. Here, far from the traditions of European royal houses and princedoms, everything could be fashioned anew. Freemasonic ideals found expression in the independence movement, and many Freemasons played decisive roles in the American struggle for independence. As well as Benjamin Franklin, there was, for example, the attorney James Otis (1725–83), who was the first to champion human rights in court. When, in 1773, settlers threw British ships' cargoes of tea into Boston Harbor in protest against the Tea Act, they were led by the Freemason Samuel Adams (1722–1803) and other members of the St. Andrew's Lodge. This action, which entered history as the "Boston Tea Party," deepened the conflict with Britain, further escalation of which after April 1775 led to the outbreak of the American War of Independence.

A bronze plaque in Boston's State Street marks the site of the Bunch of Grapes, where the first Freemasonic Lodge in Great Britain's American colonies was founded in 1733.

Washington and his "Brothers"

Thanks to the so-called "field lodges," Freemasonry was particularly widespread in the army. Many high-ranking officers were members of the fraternity. When the settlers set up an army of their own under the command of George Washington (1732–99), 20 of the 22 generals and 104 of the 106 staff officers under Washington's command were Freemasons. Washington himself had been a member of the brotherhood since 1752. During the War of Independence, when lodge brother had to fight against lodge brother, he gave the order that captured Freemasonic property must always be returned to the adversary. Following the signing of the Declaration of Independence in 1776 and its eventual recognition by the British seven years later, lodge members were instrumental in deciding the fate of the new nation. Washington himself became the first President of the United States (1789–97) and led a government that consisted exclusively of Freemasons. All 13 governors of the founding states were also lodge members. The framers of the American Constitution were likewise almost all drawn from the fraternity.

The Freemason George Washington

In 1752, George Washington was initiated into the Fredericksburg Lodge No. 1 in Virginia. In 1779, in the American Union Field Lodge, a plan was hatched, though it was never realized, to elect Washington the General Grand Master of a new Grand Lodge that would cover all the states. In 1788 he was appointed Worshipful Master of the Alexandria Lodge in Virginia. He continued to remain in office after he had become President of the United States.

Washington took the Presidential Oath of Office on the Bible from the New York St. John's Lodge No. 1. In 1793, the President laid the foundation stone of the Capitol in Washington wearing his Maryland Grand Lodge Freemason's apron.

THE ISSUE OF RACE

For more than a hundred years, a fierce debate raged within Freemasonry about the equal treatment of "colored" men.

Slaves are not Free Men

The question of whether men of every race and skin color could be admitted into lodges was a bone of contention for a long time. As regular Freemasonry had first developed in Europe and in the higher echelons of society, this question had not been relevant during the founding phase. The *Book of Constitutions* by the Scottish clergyman James Anderson states merely that "The Persons admitted Members of a Lodge must be good and true Men, free-born[…]of good report." However, at this time there were no free-born black men of good report: Under the European colonial system and in the US, black people were all slaves and servants. Black people everywhere were oppressed and had no rights. In contrast to this, Freemasonry stood for equality, fraternity, and universal human rights. This was the background against which the controversy over the admission of black men unfolded.

The Fight for Recognition

In 1784, the first lodge in the US consisting exclusively of black men was granted official recognition by the Grand Lodge of England. It was founded as the African Lodge in Boston in 1775 by the former slave Prince Hall, and in 1827 it was converted into a Grand Lodge bearing the name of its founder. While the first "colored" Grand Lodges were being founded in the US, German Freemasons, in particular, were proclaiming the principle that no candidate should be turned away

During the race riots in the US, many people were killed or wounded. This picture shows the Marine Hospital in New Orleans during the racial conflicts in Louisiana in July 1866.

It was a long time before freemasonic lodges in the US also accepted black men.

because of his skin color. For example, the German-American Freemasons' Association in New York campaigned actively for equal rights to be granted to black people, thereby arousing fierce opposition from white lodge brothers in the conservative Southern states of the US.

Angelo Soliman, the First Black Freemason in Europe

Angelo Soliman is thought to have been kidnapped from the northeast of Nigeria in 1728, when he was around seven years old; he was then trained as a valet. In 1753 he entered the service of Prince Joseph Wenzel of Liechtenstein and was soon promoted to major-domo. In 1781, Soliman was admitted to the elite Viennese *Zur wahren Eintracht* lodge, where he was eventually elected second director of ceremonies. He numbered many poets and intellectuals among his friends and spoke six languages. After his death in 1796, Soliman achieved a macabre notoriety: At the request of Emperor Franz II (1768–1835), he was stuffed and exhibited in the Viennese natural history collection until 1806.

A German-American Racial Conflict

Initially, the "white" Grand Lodges of America refused to recognize their black brothers as having equal rights. In 1857, the Grand Lodge of Massachusetts justified its refusal to admit black men into the lodges by claiming it would stir up hostility among American Freemasons.

Following the Massachusetts decision, the Hamburg Grand Lodge issued a circular, which was distributed worldwide, calling for human rights and equal treatment for black people. This circular sparked off a major row with the white Grand Lodge of New York. In 1867, the Illinois Grand Lodge, at the request of a German lodge subordinate to it, lifted the ban on admitting black men.

In 1875, the German Grand Lodges decided to recognize the Prince Hall Grand Lodge, which officially opened the doors of lodges in Germany to black men.

Thanks to the decisive support, particularly from German fraternities, for racial emancipation, the Washington Grand Lodge eventually, in 1898, had to accept that skin color was no bar to becoming a Freemason.

THE MYTH OF THE WORLD CONSPIRACY

Since its beginnings, Freemasonry has been suspected of being a conspiratorial secret society with the goal of achieving political and economic power, even of planning a global coup. It has also repeatedly been claimed that the fraternity's practices are those of a satanic cult. The originators of such allegations have never been able to provide any proof of them, and many claims have turned out to be flights of fancy.

The Basis of the Conspiracy Theories

The reasons lodges continue to be accused of conspiratorial ambitions are many. Firstly, the Masons' vow of silence fosters mistrust: If you have nothing to hide, there should be no need for secrets. The Freemasons were thus lumped together with secret societies that do not reveal their true aims. The lodges have generally remained silent about the allegations leveled against them, which has often been interpreted as an admission of guilt. Secondly, the role of the Freemasons in the French Revolution and the American War of Independence led, particularly in conservative circles, to them being branded a danger to the established order. Such conspiracy theories see the social upheavals in France and the British colonies of North America not as a reaction by large swathes of the population to social injustices, but as the work of a group of secret revolutionaries who were pulling the strings behind the scenes. The fact that influential nobles and citizens, politicians and intellectuals often socialized within the lodges provided additional fuel for the numerous conspiracy theories. Where the political, intellectual, and business elite gather behind closed doors, this always gives rise to speculation.

As a privileged minority, the Freemasons were often closely linked to the Jews by their detractors, who then construed a joint plot between "world Freemasonry" and "world Jewry." This equation of the goals of these two groups has been expressed in many conspiracy theories

since the eighteenth century and reached its peak in Nazi Germany.

Against God, Secular Rulers, and State Organizations

Time and again, individual commentators have managed to vilify the Freemasons as conspirators. One of the most influential of these was the Jesuit Abbé Augustin Barruel (1741–1821), who thought he had uncovered a threefold Freemasonic conspiracy—against God, Christianity, and the Church on the one hand; against

Anti-Freemason propaganda, especially in Nazi Germany, suggested a joint world conspiracy between the Jews and the Freemasons.

GEGEN DIE MACHT DER
GEHEIMGESELLSCHAFTEN
FREIMAURERVERBOT JA

The Freemasons' obligation to maintain secrecy, in particular, has repeatedly caused their opponents to claim that lodges were concealing their true goals.

kings and princes on the other; and finally against all bourgeois society and any form of property. Here, Barruel conflated Freemasonry and the Illuminati secret society; the Viennese linguist Leopold Alois Hoffmann (1760–1806) developed similar conspiracy theories. In the nineteenth and twentieth centuries, such notions were extrapolated and adapted to contemporary social conditions. In addition, tales concocted by former Freemasons repeatedly scared the public and governments into mobilizing against the fraternity.

The Lies of Leo Taxil

At the end of the nineteenth century, the "revelations" of the former Freemason Leo Taxil (1854–1907) caused a huge sensation. Taxil, who was actually called Gabriel Jogand-Pagès, had been dishonorably dismissed from the lodge prior to publishing several books on the Freemasons from 1885 onward. In these, he claimed that the fraternity worshipped the devil, engaged in orgies, and did not even recoil from carrying out assassinations. Taxil's writings were distributed all over the world. The Catholic Church supported Taxil and even granted him an audience with Pope Leo XIII. In 1897, Taxil "revealed" that all his allegations had been invented. The reason he gave for this hoax was that he wanted to make the Church look foolish in public.

Leo Taxil.

Ein Miniaturbild aus dem großen
Verzweiflungskampfe der römischen Priester-
herrschaft um ihren Bestand.

Unterschrift des Teufels Bitru.

Den Ostmarkdeutschen zur Lehre gezeichnet
von
Lic. theol. P. Bräunlich
Pfarrer in Weßdorf.

München.
J. F. Lehmann's Verlag.
1899.

THE ILLUMINATI

Analogous secret societies, which often had no direct links to regular Freemasonry, have contributed to bringing the brotherhood into disrepute. The Bavarian Order of the Illuminati was one such society.

Deliberate Confusion

Freemasons have faced much animosity in their barely 300-year-long history, during which they have repeatedly been held responsible for the words and deeds of other lodge affiliates and secret societies. These organizations have often deliberately used concepts and rituals similar to those of the Freemasons, so that it was easy to confuse them.

The Illuminati and Utopia

The anti-Freemason conspiracy theorist Abbé Augustin Barruel was not the only one to allege a close link between the Freemasons and the Illuminati. The secret society of the Illuminati ("enlightened ones") was founded in 1776 by the Ingolstadt-based scholar Adam Weishaupt (1748–1832).

The Illuminati took the idea of a system of initiation degrees and a vow of secrecy from the Freemasons.

Freemason and Illuminatus: The poet Johann Wolfgang von Goethe is probably the most prominent member of the Bavarian Order of the Illuminati, about which numerous conspiracy theories have circulated.

An order with its own symbols and rituals: The insignia depicted here was awarded to those Illuminati who achieved the so-called Minerval degree.

Weishaupt's ambitious plan was to create a secret school of wisdom, in which young academics could learn everything that had been banished from the curricula of the universities by the Church and the state.

With their calls for free and independent education, the Illuminati, who stood for academic progress, also criticized the ruling royal and princely houses. Unlike the Freemasons, the Order had a vision of a political and social Utopia: A world order without states, rulers, and classes, organized as a democratic republic based on the power of reason and the principle of Christian brotherly love, but that nonetheless should not be brought about by a violent revolution.

Infiltration of the Lodges

Weishaupt and the leading Illuminatus Adolph Freiherr von Knigge (1752–96), author of the book of rules of behavior entitled *Über den Umgang mit Menschen* ("On Human Relations"), deliberately attempted to infiltrate Freemasonic lodges in order to strengthen their own organization. In many cases, this plan succeeded. For example, the influential Viennese artists' lodge, *Zur*

The Ingolstadt-based scholar Adam Weishaupt founded the Order of the Illuminati in 1776. When the society was violently disbanded only nine years later, Weishaupt was forced to flee.

The End of the Illuminati

At its peak, the Order had spread throughout almost all of Austria and the German states and had between 600 and 700 members. Weishaupt, with his radical socio-political vision, voiced society's opposition to the ruling royal and princely houses, who were quick to react. The Illuminati were unjustly suspected of being the originators of the violent revolts of the French Revolution and of wanting to overthrow the Pope.

On the strength of these seditionary allegations, the Illuminati were persecuted and banned—with the support of the Roman Catholic Church—by the Elector of Bavaria, Charles Theodore (1724–99). Weishaupt was forced to flee Ingolstadt, and the Order was finally dissolved in 1785. In 1896, the Order was re-founded, and in 1925 it merged with the World League of the Illuminati.

wahren Eintracht, to which Wolfgang Amadeus Mozart and Joseph Haydn belonged, came under the influence of the Illuminati. The strong links between some lodges and the Illuminati led to both fraternities being constantly lumped together by their enemies. However, Grand Lodges, such as the Berlin Mother Lodge *Zu den drei Weltkugeln* ("Of the Three Globes"), soon recognized the intention to exploit individual Freemasonic fraternities. They distanced themselves from the Order and sent urgent warnings of Weishaupt's and Knigge's plans to the lodges affiliated to them. Despite this, the Illuminati repeatedly succeeded in initiating eminent Freemasons into their order, the most prominent surely being Johann Wolfgang von Goethe (1749–1832).

FAMOUS FREEMASONS OF THE EIGHTEENTH CENTURY

Throughout the history of Freemasonry, the organization has time-and-again attracted well-known and famous personalities drawn to its aims.

Frederick the Great and his Relations

Soon after Freemasonry had been founded, lodges in the organization's mother country, England, admitted well-known members of the nobility, such as John, Duke of Montagu, the Prince of Wales, and the Duke of Wharton, in order to raise the profile of the lodges. In Germany, the Prussian King Frederick II (1712–86) was the leading force in promoting the admission of nobles, high-ranking military officers, and influential politicians into the fraternity. For example, Frederick's younger brothers William (1722–58), Henry (1726–1802), and Ferdinand (1730–1813), who all bore the title "Prince of Prussia," also became Freemasons. Frederick's brother-in-law Ferdinand, Duke of Brunswick-Lüneburg (1721–92) and his nephew and successor as King of Prussia, Frederick William II (1744–97) also joined the society.

German-speaking Artists: Goethe, Lessing, and Mozart

Besides these, in France, Austria, and the German states, it was above all distinguished artists, personifying the spirit of the Enlightenment, who gathered in the lodges. Notable among these in Germany and Austria were Gotthold Ephraim Lessing (1729–81), Johann Wolfgang

The composer Joseph Haydn was, after Wolfgang Amadeus Mozart, the most famous German-speaking musician to join a Freemasons' lodge in the eighteenth century.

Many French freedom fighters and statesmen joined the Freemasons including, for example, the politician Gabriel Mirabeau (*above*) and the revolutionary Jean-Paul Marat.

The list of French poets and thinkers who joined lodges includes the philosopher Montesquieu (*above*), the composer Louis-Nicolas Clérambault, and the writer Helvétius.

Johann Gottfried Herder was another of the German writers and philosophers who openly professed the principles of Freemasonry and joined a lodge.

Other Famous Freemasons

François-Marie Arouet ("Voltaire") (1694–1778),
French Enlightenment writer and philosopher, known for his defence of civil liberties

John Blair (1731–1800),
American lawyer and Founding Father

James Boswell (1740–95),
Scottish lawyer and writer, best known as the biographer of Samuel Johnson

Joseph Brant (1743–1807),
Mohawk leader of the Six Nations

Giacomo Casanova (1725–98),
Italian adventurer, writer, and "entertainer"

Benjamin Franklin (1706–90),
American politician and naturalist

John Jay (1745–1829),
First Chief Justice of America

John Paul Jones (1747–92),
Naval hero of the War of Independence

John Molson (1763–1836),
Canadian entrepreneur and founder of the Molson Coors Brewing Company

Horatio Nelson (1758–1805),
English admiral of the Napoleonic Wars; victor at the Battle of Trafalgar, during which he was killed

Paul Revere (1734–1818),
American patriot and eulogized "midnight rider" of the American Revolution

Jonathan Swift (1667–1745),
Anglo-Irish writer, author of *Gulliver's Travels*

Charles Maurice de Talleyrand-Périgord (1752–1838),
French statesman

Christoph Martin Wieland (1733–1813),
German poet

John Wilkes (1725–97)
English politician and journalist

The naturalist and politician Benjamin Franklin made a decisive contribution to the lightning speed with which Freemasonry spread throughout the American colonies of the British Empire.

Louis-Nicolas Clérambault (1676–1749) to writers and philosophers like Charles de Secondat Montesquieu (1689–1755) and Claude Adrien Helvétius (1715–71). In addition, a number of important freedom fighters, politicians, and statesmen in France were also lodge members: For example, the revolutionary Jean Paul Marat (1744–93) and the politician Gabriel Mirabeau (1749–91) both belonged to the fraternity. However, it is not certain whether the revolutionary Georges Danton (1759–94) or the writer Denis Diderot (1713–84) were Freemasons. In the US, the best-known Freemasons were predominantly high-ranking officers who had been successful in the American War of Independence. Besides General (later President) George Washington (1732–99) and Major General Joseph Warren (1741–75), the latter of whom died in battle, particular mention should be made of the French-born General Marquis de Lafayette (1757–1834), who played an important role in both the War of Independence and the French Revolution. In 1789, Lafayette, who had been initiated into a field lodge in Morristown in 1779, summarized the Freemasons' fundamental principle in one sentence: "Men are born and remain free and equal in rights."

Washington or Weishaupt: Whose Face is on the Dollar?

Is the American one-dollar bill the work of Freemasons and Illuminati? This bank bill is surrounded by conspiracy theories and speculation.

The "Story of the One-Dollar Bill"

The American one-dollar bill is decorated on both sides with the "Great Seal of the United States," the official seal and national emblem of the United States of America. On the reverse of the seal there is a thirteen-step pyramid, with an "all-seeing eye" floating above it. One widespread theory states that this combination of symbols points to the Illuminati. According to this theory, the pyramid stands for the thirteen degrees of the Order. The "all-seeing eye" is a key symbol for both the Freemasons and the Illuminati. At the foot of the pyramid is the numeric combination "MDCCLXXVI," 1776 (the year the Illuminati were founded) in Roman

von Goethe (1749–1832) and Wolfgang Amadeus Mozart (1756–91). Lessing, one of the leaders of the German Enlightenment, was admitted to the Hamburg *Zu den drei Rosen* ("Of the three Roses") Lodge in 1771. Goethe belonged to the Weimar Amalia lodge from 1780. Two years later he was made Master there, and in 1783 he joined the Illuminati.

Mozart was admitted to the Vienna *Zur Wohltätigkeit* ("Benificence") lodge in 1784 and had close contacts with the artists' lodge *Zur wahren Eintracht*. It was in this famous fraternity, in 1785, that the composer Joseph Haydn also became a Freemason in Mozart's presence.

French Intelligentsia and American Generals

The list of French poets and thinkers who joined the Freemasons is also lengthy. It ranges from the composer

Cagliostro: Fraudster and Freemason

The Sicilian fraudster Guiseppe Balsamo (1743–95), who called himself Count Alessandro von Cagliostro, must qualify as the most fascinating figure among eighteenth-century Freemasons. As a magician, healer, and prophet, Cagliostro inveigled his way into polite society in Western Europe. In 1777 he is said to have been admitted into the London Esperance Lodge. He also founded his own system, the Egyptian Rite, into which he admitted women. Cagliostro founded lodges in a number of cities including The Hague, Riga, Lyon, and Basle. His lodge system, with its own rites and degrees, even succeeded in gaining a foothold in France. In 1789, he was arrested on the charge of being a Freemason by the Inquisition and sentenced to death, but in 1791 the sentence was commuted to lifetime imprisonment, and four years later Cagliostro died in an Italian jail. Goethe based the hero of his comedy *The Great Cophta* on Cagliostro. This play uses satire to criticize the dissolution of the feudal class state.

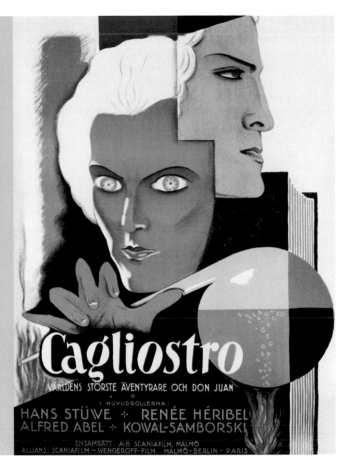

The pyramid with the all-seeing eye adorns the American official seal and the US one-dollar bill. Whether the symbols of Freemasonry necessarily indicate Freemasonry when seen elsewhere, is a matter of dispute.

numerals. It is even speculated that the person depicted on the front of the dollar bill was not George Washington at all, but the founder of the Illuminati, Adam Weishaupt, who looked rather like the President. In addition, the Freemasonic mystical number 13 appears on the bill several times.

These theories cannot be substantiated. There are simple explanations for most of the symbols on the bill: 1776 is the year of the American Declaration of Independence. The pyramid stands for strength and duration, and was never a typical Masonic symbol. The "all-seeing eye," on the other hand, is a key Masonic symbol, but was also widely used outside the lodges as a symbol of an omniscient God. There is also an explanation for the frequent use of the number 13: Thirteen colonies signed the Declaration of Independence. Incidentally, the commission that was charged with designing the Great Seal in 1776, which was then produced in 1782, contained only one Freemason besides Benjamin Franklin.

THE FREEMASONS IN THE NINETEENTH CENTURY

Freemasonry in the nineteenth century was marked by the political and industrial changes taking place in Europe and America. Moreover, the fraternity continued to be affected by conflicts and persecution.

Small Beginnings in Germany

By the end of the eighteenth century, Freemasons were once again facing bans in individual states: In 1795, the German Emperor Francis II (1768–1835) put Freemasons' lodges in Austria under police surveillance, thereby largely crushing the fraternity. In 1798, the Prussian King Frederick William III (1770–1840) introduced a law on the "prevention and punishment of secret societies," which included the Freemasons. The situation for many lodges did not improve until after 1861 when William I, a Freemason, became first King of Prussia, and then ten years later, German Emperor. The plethora of small states in Germany also meant that individual lodges were

Bonaparte (*center*) was never a Freemason, but his brothers, three of whom can be seen here at the edges of the photo, joined the fraternity.

affiliated to a many different Grand Lodges with different rites, which is one of the reasons why many Freemasons were in favor of national unity.

Encyclicals and Death Sentences

The Church also remained firmly anti-Freemasonry: Between 1821 and 1884 alone eight encyclicals against the lodges were issued. Not least because of this hostility, Freemasonry did not begin to flourish in Italy until the second half of the century—by 1889, there were no fewer than 150 lodges represented at a Freemasons' congress in Florence. The lodges that continued to suffer most from persecution were those in Portugal and Spain, where around 50 Freemasons were executed between 1810 and 1830.

Turbulence in France

Following the unification of the "Antients" and "Moderns" in 1813, Freemasonry in England enjoyed a period of steady, almost unfettered growth. The situation in France was totally different. After the suppression that followed the French Revolution, the lodges rapidly managed to reestablish themselves at the beginning of the nineteenth century. This revival was boosted by Emperor Napoleon Bonaparte (1769–1821), who sent four of his brothers to join lodges. After Napoleon was exiled, a new era of police spying began. Since many Freemasons had taken part in the revolutions of 1830 and 1848, the state authorities continued to keep an eye on the brotherhood.

In 1799, French Freemasonry, which had been split between various Grand Lodge systems, was temporarily

The Prussian king and later German emperor, William I, was a Freemason. Under his reign, the situation eased for the lodges, which had previously been persecuted in many of the small German states.

united in the amalgamative *Grand Orient de France* ("Grand Orient of France"); however, new lodge systems such as the *Grand Loge Central* ("Grand Central Lodge") kept appearing on the scene. Nonetheless, only the *Suprême Conseil* ("Supreme Council") Grand Lodge, which was founded in 1804, and the *Grand Orient* survived past the end of the century. In 1872 the Grand Lodge of Belgium struck out the invocation to the "Great Architect of the Universe" from its statutes, and five years later the Grand Orient did likewise, with the consequence that the largest French Grand Lodge was no longer recognized by the English "mother" lodge.

In the US, Freemasonry continued to expand and Freemasons remained influential in state and government. For example, in the nineteenth century alone, seven of the Presidents of the United States were members of Masonic lodges.

The long path to the goal: Freemasons had to endure many years of hostility and persecution before they eventually gained respect throughout the world.

FREEMASONRY IN THE TWENTIETH CENTURY: FROM EXPANSION TO STAGNATION

Destruction in World War II

World War II was the nadir of the recent history of European Freemasonry.

Even before the war began, all lodges had been banned in fascist Italy and in Nazi Germany, as well as in Spain and Portugal. In Italy, the persecution of Freemasons by the government of Benito Mussolini (1883–1945) had begun as early as 1923. Lodge buildings were set on fire and Freemasons were attacked, ill-treated, and killed. Freemasonry was outlawed in Italy in 1925.

In France, the Nazi-sympathizing Vichy regime dissolved all lodges in 1940, seized their assets, and auctioned off their property. In Switzerland, by contrast, the government's attempt in 1937 to ban all lodges by means of a referendum failed.

Freemasonry in the United States

Most Freemasons—estimates range between two and four million—live in the United States, where lodges have been able to develop steadily throughout the twentieth century. Attempts to form a national Grand Lodge, however, have failed thus far. North American Freemasonry does not cloak itself in secrecy: Freemasons in their typical uniform take part in parades, and lodges make their opinions on important issues publicly known. For example, the majority of the American Grand Lodges were strongly opposed to the iniquitous activities of the Ku Klux Klan, as its activities and beliefs were in sharp contrast to the Freemasonic principles of equality, fraternity, and tolerance.

Freemasonry has spread over almost the entire globe. Even Chinese lodges, like this one in London, are no longer a rarity.

Recovery

With the end of World War II, Freemasonry in Europe was able to regroup. In 1960, various Italian Grand Lodges amalgamated to form the *Grande Oriente d'Italia* ("Grand Orient of Italy"), which had around 400 affiliated lodges and approximately 15,000 members. In France, three Grand Lodges currently coexist, of which only the smallest is recognized by the English Mother Grand Lodge. The *Grand Orient de France* is estimated to have around 22,000 members, the *Grande Loge de France* ("Grand Lodge of France") just under 20,000. The number of members of the *Grande Loge Nationale Française* ("Grand National Lodge of France"), which was founded only in 1913 and initially had just two lodges under it, has risen rapidly: By the end of the twentieth century it had 210 lodges containing just under 10,000 brethren.

Calm Waters in England

In England, where the Grand Lodge is an important social institution, Freemasons' activities continued virtually unaffected during World War II. For more than 250 years, lodges have been able to develop continuously, which is why the maintenance of the rituals and charitable activities still play a substantial role in the work of British fraternities. Political involvement is frowned upon. The British King George VI (1895–1962) was a member of the Order, as are Prince Philip

Freemasons Under Socialism

Freemasonic ideas are diametrically opposed to any kind of dictatorship and are therefore almost never tolerated by absolute monarchies, fascist regimes, or in communist states. The lodges in Russia, for example, were shut down following the October Revolution of 1917, and after World War II, all lodges in the new Warsaw Pact states of Eastern Europe were banned.

The relationship of post-war Germany with Freemasonry was ambivalent. As a supporter of "historic social progress" it was accorded great respect. Nonetheless, there was no respite for the lodges banned under National Socialism. The vow of silence and the internationalism of the fraternities appear to have been ultimately irreconcilable with the theory and practice of "real socialism." The one socialist country in which the lodges were allowed to go about their business undisturbed was, and remains today, Cuba.

Only after the collapse of communist rule in Eastern Europe was a new beginning for Freemasonry possible in the Soviet Union and its former satellite states.

(1921–) and Prince Edward, Duke of Kent (1935–). At the end of the twentieth century, the United Grand Lodge was at the head of more than seven thousand lodges. There are more Freemasons in England than in any other European country, although estimations of their numbers differ wildly, ranging from 300,000–1.1 million members of the fraternity.

Persecution Under Nazism

In 1933, the Nazis ordered the dissolution of the German lodges. During World War II, Freemasonry was banned in all countries that were allied to, or occupied by the Nazis. Items seized from the lodges were put on display in anti-Masonic exhibitions; many Freemasons were also murdered.

Ludendorff's Conspiracy Theory

Extremist rightwing and nationalist propaganda was directed at Freemasons in Germany as early as the era of the Weimar Republic (1919–33). Notably, Erich Ludendorff (1865–1937), one of the leading German generals from World War I, together with his wife Mathilde (1877–1966), warned in numerous publications of an "international network" of Jews, Socialists, and Freemasons, thereby reviving the old conspiracy theories. In 1925, in fascist-ruled Italy, an assassination attempt on the head of state, Benito Mussolini, was blamed on the Freemasons so that the government could crack down on the Italian lodges; the effect of these accusations was felt in Germany, too. National Socialism adopted the accusations repeatedly leveled at Freemasonry by the Italian fascists and turned them into a hypothesis of a Freemasonic-Jewish world conspiracy. As National Socialism was opposed to any kind of humanism, ideas of equality, or internationalism, Freemasonry was also one of their targets. In addition, Hitler's regime was not prepared to tolerate an association that was not under Nazi leadership and control, and that moreover had secrecy as one of its most important principles.

A Lodge in a Concentration Camp

In 1943, there was a unique incident in the history of Nazi concentration camps: In the Esterwegen camp in Emsland, members of the Belgian resistance founded the Freemasonic lodge *Liberté chérie* ("Cherished Liberty"). In November 2004, a monument was erected on the memorial site in Esterwegen in honor of these prisoners.

Responsible for everything: The fascist heads of state Adolf Hitler and Benito Mussolini spread the rumor of a world conspiracy of Jews and Freemasons and had lodges dissolved.

The Dissolution of the Lodges

From the 1920s onward, the Nazis' chief ideologist, Alfred Rosenberg (1893–1946), worked vehemently as a propagandist. He even alleged that the Freemasons had deliberately precipitated World War I. The first step in the battle against Freemasonry consisted of excluding Freemasons from membership of the National Socialist Party (NSDAP). After 1931, the gradual dissolution of the lodges began, accompanied by wholesale attacks on Freemasons by the paramilitary brownshirts (the *Sturmabteilung*, "Stormtroopers," or SA).

Many lodges attempted to escape the threat of dissolution by emphasizing their absolute loyalty to the Nazi state, and renaming themselves German-Christian Orders. However, these attempts at assimilation were unsuccessful. In July 1935, three Old Prussian Grand Lodges disbanded themselves before the general ban on Freemasonry was announced in August 1935. The expansion of Nazi rule in Europe led to the crushing of Freemasonry in occupied countries as well.

Unlike Jews, former Freemasons in the Third Reich were not systematically exterminated. There are 62 known cases of German Freemasons—of whom there are estimated to have been around 80,000—being murdered by the state. These include the SPD politician Julius Leber (1891–1945) and the journalist Carl von Ossietzky (1889–1938), although they were persecuted for resisting National Socialism, not for Freemasonry.

After the end of the war, the slow process of rebuilding the German lodges began. Of the ten Grand Lodges that had existed prior to Nazi rule, three were revived. In 1958, the remaining lodges combined to form the *Vereinigte Großlogen von Deutschland* ("United Grand Lodges of Germany"). Today it is estimated that the number of members in their affiliated lodges stands at between 13,000 and 21,000.

The journalist and Freemason Carl von Ossietzky was a fervent critic of National Socialism. In 1938, this Nobel Prize winner died of tuberculosis following gross ill-treatment by the Nazis.

The Nazis used posters to stoke up the campaign against Freemasons. Hitler's Germany banned the lodges as early as 1935.

CRIMINAL LODGES

The secret terrorist activities of the Italian *Propaganda Due* lodge came out in 1981, and opponents of Freemasonry saw this as confirming their conspiracy theories.

Countering the Left

International Freemasonry has been brought into disrepute by one lodge in particular, the *Propaganda Due* lodge, P2 for short, which was founded in Rome in 1887 and was never a regular Masonic fraternity. The lodge, which prior to its temporary dissolution admitted only selected politicians, writers, and scholars, was reestablished in 1944 by the mattress-maker Licio Gelli (1919–). In order to gain influence in Italian politics, Gelli, who was Worshipful Master of the lodge from 1967, attempted to bring together top politicians, leaders of industry, military commanders, and high-ranking policemen, as well as employees of various secret services, hoping to prevent the feared swing to the Left and electoral success for the Communist Party in Italy.

Criminal intrigues behind closed doors: From time to time, the police have had to step in when lodges have attempted to put themselves beyond the law in order to secure power.

Strategy of Tension

The high point of the lodge's activities came in the 1970s, when the leadership was involved in numerous criminal and terrorist activities as part of its "strategy of tension." This strategy depended on using acts of terror, the blame for which was laid at the door of other organizations, to create a climate of fear among the public. Such destabilization was intended to drive voters into the arms of the parties of the Right, standing for "law and order," and create the conditions necessary for a coup d'etat. Members of the lodge are thought to have been involved in the bombing of the "Italicus" express train in 1974 and in the bomb attack on Bologna railway station, which killed 85 people in 1980. According to a

statement by Richard Brenneke, an employee of the American and Israeli secret services, the US Government provided financial support of up to ten million dollars a month for *Propaganda Due*.

962 Well-Known Members

As early as 1974, before the conspiratorial nature of the lodge became known, the *Grande Oriente d'Italia* decided to close it down, but was unable to implement this decision. In May 1981, the conspiracy was discovered during a search of Licio Gelli's house. During this raid, a list of the members of P2 was found, containing the

Scandals in America and in England

In 1826, Freemasonry in North America was rocked by a severe crisis: The kidnapping and alleged murder of the anti-Masonic author William Morgan (1774–circa 1826) was blamed on lodge brethren and unleashed a wave of hostility in the United States. An Anti-Freemason Party was formed, and many lodges disbanded.

In 1988, in Great Britain, Freemasons were linked to a series of scandals in the British police force relating to bribery, cover-ups, and corruption. Because the police was seen as having been infiltrated by Freemasons, the British Home Secretary attempted to force members of the police to declare their lodge membership. The Freemasons successfully resisted this attempt, and the corruption cases were never fully cleared up. However, the scandal provided fresh fuel for the theories about the dubious intrigues of Freemasons.

names of 962 well-known personalities from politics, the military, business, and the secret services. The most prominent member, entered as number 1,816, was the media mogul and future Italian Prime Minister, Silvio Berlusconi. In 1982, the Italian parliament declared the dissolution of this criminal lodge. A parliamentary investigative commission concluded in its final report merely that the aim of the secret society had been the infiltration of the government rather than a direct seizure of power or coup. However, a court of lay assessors in Bologna later came to the conclusion that P2 was directly involved in right-wing terrorist activity and was planning to overthrow the government, crush the trade unions, and infiltrate the media.

The name of the current Italian Prime Minister, Silvio Berlusconi, was one of those on the list of members of *Propaganda Due* that was seized in a raid in 1981.

FAMOUS FREEMASONS OF THE NINETEENTH AND TWENTIETH CENTURIES

In the nineteenth and twentieth centuries, too, famous people from all walks of life were admitted to Freemasonic lodges. As Freemasons are not obliged to reveal the fact of their membership of the fraternity, any listing of famous Freemasons is bound to be incomplete.

Freemason Presidents of the United States

George Washington (1732–99),
Period of office 1789–97
James Monroe (1758–1831),
Period of office 1817–25
Andrew Jackson (1767–1845),
Period of office 1829–37
James Knox Polk (1795–1849),
Period of office 1845–49
James Buchanan (1791–1868),
Period of office 1857–61
Andrew Johnson (1808–75),
Period of office 1865–69
James Garfield (1831–81),
Period of office 1881
William McKinley (1843–1901),
Period of office 1897–1901
Theodore Roosevelt (1858–1919),
Period of office 1901–09
William Taft (1857–1930),
Period of office 1909–13
Warren Harding (1865–1923),
Period of office 1921–23
Franklin D. Roosevelt (1882–1945),
Period of office 1933–45
Harry S. Truman (1884–1972),
Period of office 1945–53
Lyndon B. Johnson (1908–73),
Period of office 1963–69
Gerald R. Ford (1913–2006),
Period of office 1974–77

A–Z of Freemasons

Salvador Allende (1908–73), President of Chile, Freemason from 1929.

The Italian freedom fighter Giuseppe Garibaldi

The first Turkish President, Mustafa Kemal Atatürk

Roald Amundsen (1872–1928), Norwegian polar explorer, was the first person to reach both the North and South poles.

Louis Armstrong (1900–71), jazz musician. Armstrong is said to have been a member of Montgomery Lodge No. 18 in New York.

Mustafa Kemal Atatürk (1881–1939), father of modern Turkey. Until his death, was a member of the *Macedonia Resorta et Veritas* lodge.

Simon Bolivar (1783–1830), leader of the South American independence movement.

Ludwig Börne (1786–1837), German writer and friend of Heinrich Heine. Was admitted to the Frankfurt *Zur aufgehenden Morgenröthe* lodge in 1809.

Winston Churchill (1874–1965), Prime Minister of the United Kingdom. Was admitted in 1901 to the London United Studholme Lodge No. 1591.

The discoverer of penicillin, Sir Alexander Fleming

Musician and composer Duke Ellington

Charles Dickens (1812–70), English author of *Oliver Twist* and *Great Expectations*.

Sir Arthur Conan Doyle (1859–1930), English writer, creator of Sherlock Holmes. From 1893 Master of Phoenix Lodge No. 257 in Portsmouth.

Duke Ellington (1879–1974), American jazz musician and composer. From 1923 was a "Prince Hall" Freemason in Washington's Social Lodge No. 1.

Sir Alexander Fleming (1891–1955), discoverer of penicillin, Grand Steward and Junior Grand Warden of the United Grand Lodge of England.

Henry Ford (1863–1947), the founder of the Ford factory became Master of the Detroit Palestine Lodge No. 357 in 1894 and shortly before his death joined Zion Lodge No. 1.

Clark Gable (1901–60), the male lead in the film *Gone With The Wind* was admitted to Beverly Hills Lodge No. 528 in 1933.

Giuseppe Garibaldi (1807–82), Italian statesman and freedom-fighting hero. Was admitted to a French lodge in Montevideo in 1844, and in 1864 became Grand Master of Italy.

Heinrich Heine (1797–1856), German writer admitted to the Paris Craft lodge *Les Trinosophes* in 1844.

Charles Lindberg (1902–74), aviation pioneer. Lindberg became a member of Keystone Lodge No. 243 in St. Louis in 1926. He is thought to have taken his Masonic documents with him on his famous transatlantic crossing.

Franz Liszt (1811–86), German composer, admitted to the Frankfurt *Zur Einigkeit* lodge in 1841.

Gustav Stresemann (1878–1929), German Chancellor and Nobel Peace Prize winner. He was admitted to the *Friedrich der Große* lodge in Berlin in 1923.

Kurt Tucholsky (1890–1935), German journalist and writer, joined the Berlin *Zur Morgenröthe* lodge in 1924 and shortly afterward the Paris *L'Effort* lodge.

Mark Twain (1835–1910), the creator of Tom Sawyer and Huckleberry Finn was actually called Samuel L. Clemens. In 1861, he was admitted to the Polar Star Lodge in Missouri.

John Wayne (1907–79), in 1970 the movie star and director joined the Marion McDaniel Lodge No. 56 in Tucson, Arizona.

Oscar Wilde (1854–1900), Irish poet, writer, and author of *The Picture of Dorian Gray*.

FREEMASONRY TODAY

Freemasonry has succeeded in spreading across the world and today has several million members, although due to the large numbers of irregular lodges, it is very difficult to accurately estimate numbers. Many lodges complain of declining and aging memberships.

Lodges in 100 Countries Around the World

Today, there are regular Freemasonic lodges in approximately 100 countries. Since there is no comprehensive listing, their number, as well as the number of brethren, can only be guessed at. At the beginning of the millennium the latter were thought to number between 3.5 and 6 million. This lack of clarity is exacerbated by a network of regular and irregular (i.e. not recognized by the Grand Lodge of England) fraternities that is impenetrable to the layperson. Three-quarters of all Freemasons in France are members of irregular lodges; in Belgium and Italy the proportion stands at well above 90 percent.

Estimated Numbers of Regular Freemasons Around the World

Worldwide: 3–6 million
US 2–3 million
UK 450,000–660,000
Brazil circa 200,000
Canada 120,000–160,000
Australia 90,000–200,000
France 84,000
Ireland 38,000–50,000
Mexico 28,000
Cuba 22,000–28,000
New Zealand 20,000–25,000
Germany 12,000–20,000
Sweden, Norway, the Philippines, and India each have 10,000–15,000

In Belgium, only the *Grand Loge Régulière de Belge* ("Grand Regular Lodge of Belgium"), in Spain only the *Gran Logia d'España* ("Grand Lodge of Spain"), and in Italy only the lodge of the economics professor Giuliano Di Bernardo, are officially recognized. The venerable Grand Orients of France (1773), Spain (1780), Portugal (1802), Belgium (1833), and Italy (1864) are all irregular.

Freemasons in Africa and Asia

It is not just Europe, the US, Canada, Australia, and various South and Central American countries that have regular fraternities. There are also regular Grand Lodges in eight African countries—Benin, Burkina Faso, Gabon, Guinea, Ivory Coast, Liberia, Mali, and Togo. A further dozen African countries have many lodges working under the three Grand Lodges of England, Scotland, and Ireland. In South Africa alone there are thought to be almost 500 regular and irregular lodges. The situation in Asia, where India, the Philippines, Taiwan, Japan, Singapore, Hong Kong, and Sri Lanka are thought to be strongholds of Freemasonry, is difficult to ascertain.

Too Much Tradition, Too Little Future?

More than half of all Freemasons today live in the United States. However, there are indications that numbers are declining rapidly. For example, the research group of the Swiss *Alpina* ("Alpine") Grand Lodge has found that the number of Freemasons in the US has fallen from 4.1 million lodge brethren in around 1960 to 2.1 million today. Worldwide, the fraternity, according to its own figures, has lost more than half of its members in the past 30 years. Even the oldest Grand Lodge of all, the United Grand Lodge of England, is thought to have suffered a dramatic drop in membership numbers since 1970—believed to be as many as 275,000.

One reason for the declining membership figures frequently cited by both Freemasons and their critics, is that the lodges have a great tradition, but no vision for the future. Many lodges bemoan their aging membership,

The future of the lodges (this picture shows a Masonic Hall in Mexico) is uncertain. Many fraternities complain about declining membership; others feel that the values of Freemasonry are more important than ever.

saying that it is very difficult to enthuse young men about the ideas of the fraternity. During its almost 300-year-long history, Freemasonry has hardly modernized at all: Its goals, symbols and rituals have remained almost unchanged, and many people see it as a relic of times long past.

Ancient Goals, New Relevance

Many Freemasons, on the other hand, emphasize the fact that their ancient goals have acquired a new topicality in the modern world. In an anonymous society characterized by competitiveness and the economic pursuit of profit, the values of humanity, tolerance, solidarity, and friendship, and last but not least, the pursuit of self-improvement, are more important than ever.

Some recent publications, therefore, talk of the need for a "new Enlightenment."

BIBLIOGRAPHY

Baigent, Michael, and Richard Leigh. *The Temple and The Lodge*. London: Arrow, 2006.

Bradley, Michael. *The Secrets of the Freemasons*. New York: Sterling, 2008.

Cooper, Robert L. D. *Cracking the Freemasons Code*. New York: Atria, 2007.

Hagger, Nicholas. *The Secret Founding of America*. London: Watkins, 2009.

Hodapp, Christopher. *Freemasons for Dummies*. Hoboken: Wiley, 2005.

Hodapp, Christopher. *Solomon's Builders: Freemasons, Founding Fathers and the Secrets of Washington, DC*. Berkeley: Ulysses Press, 2006.

Jeffers, Paul H. *The Freemasons in America*. New York: Citadel, 2007.

Jones, Bernard E. *Freemasons' Guide and Compendium*. Nashville: Cumberland House, 2006.

Poll, Michael R. *The Freemasons Key*. New Albany: Cornerstone, 2008.

Ridley, Jasper. *The Freemasons*. New York: Arcade, 2002.

Tabbert, Mark. *American Freemasons*. New York: NYU Press, 2006.

Young, John K., and Barb Karg. *The Everything Freemasons Book*. Cincinnati: Adams Media, 2006.

PICTURE CREDITS

INDEX